IS YOUR GLASS LAUGH FULL?

SOME THOUGHTS ON SEEING THE HUMOR IN LIFE

Ronald P. Culberson

Gilbert Belle
Press

Gilbert Belle Press
Herndon, Virginia

Is Your Glass Laugh Full?
Some Thoughs on Seeing the Humor in Life

Published by: Gilbert Belle Press
Herndon, Virginia

Cover design by Dunn & Associates Design
Author photo by Frasier Photography
Text layout by Ad Graphics, Inc.

Printed in the United States of America

ISBN: 0-9754077-0-8

For information or to order: (703) 742-8812 or www.FUNsulting.com

*This book is dedicated
to my loving wife Wendy
who is my reason for living
and to CC and Ryan,
the most wonderful children
I have ever known.*

Contents

Acknowledgments

A number of people helped me with this book either purpose-fully or inadvertently.

Trisha Medved was the first to suggest that I consider writing a book. Although she may regret that advice, she has been a willing resource and great cousin-in-law ever since. Sam Horn gave me encouragement, sound guidance and let me know that my voice was always worth putting in print. Steve Cohn performed more edits than I deserved and if you find any errors in the text, it's because I changed his corrections. Mariah Burton Nelson has always been a good friend, an encourager of my writing and someone who always gave me valuable feedback whether I wanted to hear it or not.

My mastermind groups continually prompted me to "just get it done" and even suggested a successful financial penalty for every month I didn't write. For that I am grateful to Bill Cates, Willie Jolley, Steven Gaffney, Wolf Rinke, Jim Ball, Arnold Sanow, Rick Maurer and Lynne Waymon.

I am so lucky to have mentors who are willing to work with me. Lou Heckler has given me such good advice on the craft of story telling. I only hope that one day I command the platform as he does. Mark LeBlanc has helped me understand my business and to focus on that which will not only give me financial success but keep my "fun meter" on max.

Michael Aronin will look for his name here, so I better thank him too. He is a great friend, a trusted advisor and someone who "gets it" when no one else does. He's also pretty darn funny.

My nephews Adam and Wes did a ton of research for another book that I never wrote. I promised them a mention in the book so I wouldn't have to pay them very much. Here it is.

Midd Hunt and Rich Frasier, my videographer and photographer, make me look good when no one else can. They are also good friends who will not hesitate to point out both my physical and psychological shortcomings. Luckily my faults pale in comparison to theirs. Nonetheless, I need friends like that to keep me humble and sane.

The lobby of the Hyatt hotel at Dulles Airport was my regular writing refuge. General Manger and friend Jim Deuel welcomed me everytime I showed up. He also gave me a great deal for two days in a tenth floor room with a view. It was there that I finished my first draft.

I thank all of the people mentioned in this book. Most were given the opportunity to review their chapters and they offered very little criticism and lots of support. The ones that offered lots of criticism are no longer in the book. So there.

Most of all, I thank my wife for being my biggest fan. No matter what, she is cheering me on, offering suggestions and making me feel important. She is the reasonable voice when I lose my own perspective and her laugh is my grandest prize. She is my best friend and I love her very much.

Finally, I am grateful for the gift of humor and the many other blessings I have received from God. I am a lucky guy.

IS YOUR GLASS
LAUGH FULL?

It's More Than Just A-Muse

An Introduction to Seeing Your Glass Laugh Full

*It is my belief; you cannot deal with
the most serious things in the world unless
you understand the most amusing.*
– Winston Churchill, Prime Minister

I was born with a gift. It's not one of those super extraordinary gifts like in the movie *Rainman,* where Dustin Hoffman's character can tell you what day July 7th will be in 2052, but it is a valuable gift nonetheless. On top of having most of my original teeth, being able to match my tie to my suit, and being schooled in Southern manners, I was blessed with the gift of humor.

Now let's get this straight. I am not a stand-up comedian and I don't write a daily column in the Washington Post (although that would be nice). But I do have an ability to see the humor in everyday situations.

Here's an example: Just the other day, during a workshop I was conducting, a woman told an embarrassing story of getting to work and finding a pair of her husband's underwear in her briefcase. My immediate response to this was, "Well, it was a *brief case!*" OK, so maybe you think I should return this gift. Regardless, it *has* been a blessing in my life.

I'm 42 years old. I own a great speaking business. I am a Rotarian, an active member of the Chamber of Commerce, and the president of a local association. I'm a former Deacon and Elder in my church. I'm a parent. I'm a husband. For all intents and purposes, I have a good life.

It's not likely I'll be featured on the cover of *Time* magazine anytime soon, but I have the privilege of doing many wonderful things in my life. I love my job. I love my family and I love life. And you know what I think is the secret to all this? Humor.

I know. You're thinking, "You're not that funny." You may be right; yet just about everyone around me thinks I am. In fact, if you ask anyone who knows me what my gift is, they'll say humor.

So what is this gift all about? That's what I want to tell you. It's the ability to see humor when and where most people can't. This gift allows me to bring a bit of lightheartedness into some of the most serious situations. Instead of seeing the glass half-full or half-empty as the saying goes, I tend to see it *laugh* full. It is this ability to see the balance of serious and humorous that makes my life rich. And you can develop that ability.

Let me give you an example.

Mary

In the fall of 1987, I was in my second year as a hospice home care social worker. As a member of an interdisciplinary team of health care professionals, I was expected to attend to the psychosocial concerns of people who were terminally ill and to be a source for support to their families.

On a beautiful October day, I arrived at the home of Mary Burton (not her real name), a 68-year-old wife and mother of three. Mary had been married to her husband Joe for nearly 50 years. Her three daughters were grown and each had a family and a successful career. Mary was a loving parent and was the major reason for her family's success. Mary was also dying of cancer and had been given less than six months to live. As I arrived at Mary's house that day, I had no idea she would teach me one of the greatest lessons I would ever learn.

Joe welcomed me at the door and politely escorted me into Mary's bedroom. He then excused himself so Mary and I could get better acquainted. Mary was neatly perched on her bed, anxiously awaiting her afternoon "visitor." Her face lit up as I entered the room and she invited me to sit down and "make myself comfortable." It did not take long for me to understand why Mary was the love of her family.

As I sat in Mary's room that day, I saw first hand the significant role she played in her family's life. She loved her husband and cared for him as if he were breakable. She did this, not in a smothering way, but the way you treasure something valuable. She loved her children, and while she gave of herself freely to them, it was clear she had also provided firm yet understanding discipline. I recognized this by the way in which she and her family showed so much respect and courtesy to me *and* to each other. She spoke fondly of her life and expressed satisfaction in the way it all "turned out." At the same time, she expressed sincere respect for her illness and hoped her current state of relative well-being would last so she could savor the time with her loved ones. After about 45 minutes of conversation, I asked to talk with Joe and the one daughter, Jill, who was there at the time of my visit. They shared their sense of grief at the thought of losing Mary and yet they showed a strength that clearly came from her.

I left Mary's house that day feeling confident that she and her family would get through this difficult experience as we are all supposed to — by leaning on the shoulders of those we love. And since Mary was doing rather well, despite her illness, I looked forward to her family using the next few months to build upon their already strong relationships.

Two weeks after my visit, Mary was admitted to the hospice inpatient unit, a unit reserved for patients in crisis or near death. Apparently, she had taken a dramatic turn for the worse in the previous two days. Her doctor thought this episode was unrelated to her illness due to its sudden onset and assumed it was either a reaction to her medication or a virus. To be on the safe side, he admitted her to the hospice unit so he and the nursing staff could monitor her more closely.

The Hospice of Northern Virginia inpatient unit was a beautifully renovated school building which opened in 1982 as one of the first hospice inpatient facilities in the country. It was a lovely setting complete with hardwood floors, flowered sheets and colorful wallpaper. The setting was intended to seem more homelike, even though it functioned as an acute care hospital.

The moment I walked into Mary's hospice room, I realized her situation had changed dramatically for the worse. The color in her face was gone. Her listless body sunk into the mattress as though she had no strength.

As I approached, a comforting look of recognition warmed her face. I took her frail hand in mine and asked, "How are you doing?"

"Not good," she whispered.

"Are you getting what you need?"

"They're spoiling me." she said with a weak grin. "The nurses have been so nice—they seem to anticipate my every need."

Then Mary rose up on her elbows, took a long look around the room and announced, "This place is beautiful. I had heard so much about it, *I was dying to see it!*"

I froze, not knowing how to respond.

Mary closed her eyes, fell back on her pillow and let loose a weak burst of laughter.

"Can you believe I said that?" she asked, shaking her head in disbelief. We laughed together while I marveled at her brave use of humor in the face of such daunting circumstances.

Six hours later, Mary died.

Mary had it. She had the balance. She knew she was dying, or else the comment would not have been so funny. Yet she allowed herself to enjoy a moment of fun. She saw her glass *laugh* full and appreciated the humor where others would have been afraid to acknowledge it, much less say it out loud. As a result, she experienced all the situation had to offer. It was rich.

Humor Is the Ticket to Happiness

"We don't laugh because we're happy, we're happy because we laugh," said William James, the eighteenth century philosopher and psychologist. As you will see, the nature of humor is to change our thinking and turn it upside down. It helps us to see the ups during the downs in our life. Our happiness depends on seeing through the adversity, despair and tragedies of the world around us to that which is positive, healing and healthy. Humor is not the only way to achieve this but is one of the most effective and affective ways I have found. It's fulfilling *and* fun.

We live in a time when the world is battling adversity around every turn. Many of us see our glasses as half-empty. Now, more than ever, we need a bright spot that outlasts the darkness. Humor is the way we keep our sanity while focusing on what's important. It's the *fun* in funeral, the *ha* in hazardous, and the *yuk* in yucky that makes life bearable.

For me, humor has been the ticket to happiness. Yet it's not just about the humor. It is humor coupled with other personality qualities such as compassion, integrity, and responsibility. When you think of someone like Bill Cosby, Erma Bombeck, or Garrison Keillor, what comes to mind? Humor, right? But there is something else.

They exude a goodness that comes from the heart. It's not just the humor that works. It's the combination of the humanness and the humor-ness. It's a potent formula for a good life: Good humor = a good life. Through the stories in this book, I would like to show you how it works so that you can bring a little more humor into your life.

There is no *one* secret to a fulfilling and balanced life. If there was, best-selling author Stephen Covey would have already found it! The secret is in the way we live and the way we laugh.

Your life is up to you. But if you are willing to take this journey with me, I can guarantee, based on years of experience and my good fortune of working with thousands of people across the United States, this philosophy works—if you apply it.

Let me ask you to do these things. Read this book for its entertainment value. Enjoy the stories. Ponder the quotes. Consider the ideas. Then, think about the ways the information applies to you. My hope is that these ideas will help you live a rich, full, and happy life. Why? Because if you are happy, you tend to make the people around you happy. If the people around you are happy, they may come into contact with me! See, it all comes full circle.

I truly believe that adding humor to your daily routine at home, at work, and in your community can have a profound impact on the way your life turns out.

Oscar Wilde, the nineteenth century writer said, "Life is much too important a thing ever to talk seriously about it." Are you ready to talk seriously about how the power of seeing *your* glass *laugh* full can help you lead a good life? Then let's go.

PART I

YOU DON'T HAVE TO BE SERIOUS IF YOU'RE GOOD!

Kiddie College

If no one ever took risks, Michelangelo
would have painted the Sistine floor.

– Neil Simon, playwright

A participant in one of my presentations once said to me, "You don't understand. I have a lot of responsibility. I have lots of pressure on me to produce. I can't have fun at my work. No one would take me seriously. I would lose the respect of my staff." The longer he went on, the less I respected him. Seriously. I couldn't imagine working for or with him. I got depressed just thinking about it.

Being serious does not make you respectable. I don't mean to suggest that if you're serious you're despicable; I'm just saying that serious is not the same as respect. Ever wonder why are we so obsessed with being serious? Do you realize we are groomed for seriousness from the minute we're born?

Will you please grow up?

Stop being silly.

Act your age!

Don't make fun. It's not nice.

You better wipe that smile off your face.

Do these scolding phrases sound familiar? The sad thing is we grow up thinking we must be serious to succeed. What happened to laughing all the way to the bank? Is laughter really the best medicine? Does she who laughs last?' And if you smile, does the whole world really smile with you, or is everyone secretly thinking, *He doesn't take me seriously*? Maybe Norman Cousins didn't really cure himself with laughter. Maybe it was all done on a sound stage in the middle of the Arizona desert. No wait. That was the lunar landing. Nonetheless, we're way too serious.

For instance, in 2003 when Al Gore appeared on *Saturday Night Live*, he broke his own mold. In one skit, he was shirtless in a hot tub with a Joe Lieberman impersonator parodying the reality TV show *The Bachelor*. It was hysterical and was "soooo not Al Gore" according to my daughter. I remember saying to my wife at the time (at the time of the show, not that I have a different wife now), "He must not be running for President." The next day, he announced he wasn't running.

How did I know? Any idiot (and that's how I knew) realized that if Al Gore was going to run for president, he could not do something "silly" on *Saturday Night Live*. The American public would not tolerate it. Instead, they expect him to *act his age* and *grow up*.

My point is simply this. Your "elders" have probably convinced you that you need to be serious—to be taken seriously. I'm telling you that's not necessarily so. If you would instead focus on being excellent at your job, excellent at your role and responsibilities as a partner, excellent at your duties on the fundraising committee or excellent at setting an example as a parent, you will earn the confidence and respect of others.

Being excellent at what you do will get you places. Being excellent *and* being funny at the same time will get you even farther. Being serious without being excellent isn't going to take you anywhere.

In third grade, I had an opportunity to appear on *Kiddie College*, a competitive quiz show for third graders on WCYB-

TV, the local NBC affiliate. How many third-graders get to appear on TV? This was the big time. Mrs. Hicks told our class she would pick the three students to represent Meadowview Elementary based on the scores of a multiple choice quiz. We had to complete 50 questions in 30 minutes. Being the stellar student I was, I immediately calculated that I would have approximately one minute, twenty-four seconds per question!

Piece of cake. This should be a breeze.

Mrs. Hicks distributed the quiz and I confidently began answering the questions. After ten minutes, I had completed ten questions. I was ahead of the clock.

Wait a minute. That's not right.

I felt a drop of sweat roll down my lip. I had goofed big time. I had divided 30 into 50 rather than 50 into 30. I had 40 questions left and only 20 minutes to finish them.

Drat.

For a split second, I thought about cheating. But whenever I considered breaking the rules, I heard my father's voice in my head warning me against the perils of not doing the right thing. I was convinced I'd either go blind or my mother would break her back if I cheated. So, I put it in high gear and cranked through the questions.

As I circled the letter "B" on the last question, the alarm clock on Mrs. Hicks' desk rang.

Done.

I may not have gotten all the questions correct, but I finished.

The next day, Mrs. Hicks read the names of the three people who had the best scores on the quiz.

"Martha Turley. Becky Wohlford. Ronnie Culberson."

Yes, Becky Wohlford and Martha Turley and I would proudly represent Meadowview Elementary School with the goal of taking home free Moore's potato chips (the show's sponsor), $50 cash for our school and the deep respect and admiration of our peers.

Unlike the contestants on *Jeopardy,* we did not study, practice or mentally prepare for *Kiddie College*. Instead, we went shopping for new clothes. Heck, we were going to be on television. We had to look good.

On the big night, the tension was thick. We attended the pre-competition instruction session where we were briefed on the sequence of questioning and the scoring process. I was distracted by how cute Becky looked, all dressed up. Becky and I were kinda "boyfriend and girlfriend," at least in my mind. I know that seems odd, but we did grow up in the Appalachian Mountains!

The show started with a quick round of introductions. The host asked us to introduce ourselves, give our ages and say what our fathers did for a living.

"My name is Ronnie Culberson, I'm eight years old and my dad works at Emory & Henry College," I said, and I made sure to lean into the microphone so my family watching at home could hear me.

"What does your father do at Emory and Henry College?" the host asked.

Wait a minute. I didn't prepare for this line of questioning. I'm eight. How am I supposed to know the specifics of my father's job? I don't even know why he has to work.

"I'm not sure, he just goes there every day," I said, still leaning into the microphone so everyone could hear.

The studio audience (our parents) giggled, the host smiled and then he moved on.

I later found out everyone thought my dad had some type of embarrassing job—like he was a janitor and I didn't want to admit it. I think my parents spent the next two weeks clearing up the misunderstanding. I was terribly embarrassed that we hadn't even started the tough questions and I was already behind in the scoring.

The show consisted of three rounds of questions alternating between teams. The team with the best score won and then came back the next week to compete against another school.

The first round began. Becky was first, I was second and Martha was third. Apparently we had to sit boy-girl even on game shows. The host asked Becky to identify the temperature at surface of the sun.

I must have misheard him. Surely we were not going to get questions of that level. Who could answer that? (Author's note: In hindsight and in the spirit of telling a good story, I have realized my memory may have exaggerated these questions a bit. Isn't it interesting that the more we tell a story, the more details we remember!)

"11,000 degrees Fahrenheit." Becky nailed the answer! We clapped, hooted and raised our arms above our heads. We didn't give each other high fives since there was no such thing as high fives back then. On top of that, I'm not sure Martha or Becky would have touched me.

The other team missed their first question. *Not too smart,* I thought.

I prepared to go in for the kill.

The host turned to me said, "Mr. Culberson, how many ounces in a pound of butter?"

What's this? Culinary Arts? I don't know anything about cooking. I'm a boy. Boys aren't taught to cook. We go to shop class or play sports. I'm no Bobby Crocker!

Think. Think. What do you know about butter? Well, we usually got Parkay. In the commercial, the tub says 'butter' and the actor says, 'Parkaaaay.' But we had sticks, not a tub and the blue box came with four sticks

That's it! It's so obvious. What a simple question after all.

"Four," I said as I leaned into the microphone. Then, I froze in a serious contemplative pose.

Wrong answer.

"BZZZZZZZZZZZZZZZZZZZZZZZZZZZZZZZZZZZZZZZZZZZZ ZZZZZZZZZZZZZZZZZ!"

The buzzer sounds much louder in person.

Wrong? How could it be wrong?

I looked at Becky. Disgust. I looked at Martha but she wouldn't look at me. I couldn't see my parents but I had an idea they were hiding their faces, thinking my dad just might end up in a janitorial job after all.

"It's sixteen. There are sixteen ounces in a pound, stupid." Becky said.

"Oh."

She didn't look as cute anymore with that vein raising the skin on her forehead. I slumped a bit and started to focus. *I've got to get serious about this.*

At the end of the first round it was two to two. Martha had correctly answered her question and the other team had aced their remaining questions.

We began round two. I was first on my team.

I hope they don't ask me what my mother does for a living.

Mr. Culberson, "what is nine times nine?"

Under my desk, I counted on my fingers.

"Eighty one?" I asked with a rise in my voice that told everyone I was asking a question rather than answering one.

The silence was deafening.

"Ding."

The bell! The bell! I didn't get the buzzer. I got it ri-ight, I got it ri-ight!

Becky and Martha politely clapped.

How could they be so calm when I was about to wet my pants? This is what it's all about. I had scored. Nirvana.

At the end of round two, the score was four to three in our favor. Martha had missed her question but two people on the other team missed their questions.

We were in the lead heading into round three. Martha went first.

The host began, "Miss Turley, what is the speed at impact of a bowling ball dropped from 300 feet taking into consideration a thirty mile-per-hour upwind?" At least that's what I *remember* the question was.

What am I doing here? How did I get picked to do this? Someone must have forged the quiz Mrs. Hicks gave me.

Martha answered the question correctly. I didn't even hear her answer. I was stunned. I looked at her as if she were Einstein. How could she get so much smart in such a little head?

The other team answered their question and then it was Becky's turn.

"Miss Wohlford, what is the square root of 375 times 438 carried out to two decimal points?"

"Eight thousand, four hundred eighty one, point eight three." (OK, just work with me here to enjoy the story.)

Becky did the calculations in her head! She and Martha winked at each other. Winked! Like they had this special brainiac club with a secret algebra password. And boys like me weren't allowed. Meanwhile, I'm starting to taste remnants of my dinner. Little pieces of beanie weenies are working their way up my esophagus. "We want out," they were chanting.

Just keep it together. You'll be fine. They have to be out of hard questions.

The other team answered correctly.

My turn again.

What if I throw up? Would they disqualify me or just make me come back after I cleaned up? I have to maintain control— I have to take this seriously.

"Mr. Culberson. What do you call a place where rocks and gravel are dug out of the ground?"

Oh great. Becky lives about 50 feet from one of these places and I get the question. When we used to play there, we would watch the trucks going in and out full of gravel. I can picture it—it is a big hole in the ground with rock walls all around it.

They blast and dig the stone out. But what's it called? It's not a mine because it's not underground. So what the heck is it?

"You have five seconds, Mr. Culberson."

What is it? What is it? Warning, stage three alert. You're losing it. You have to answer something.

"Uh, yes, it's called a Rock Digging Place."

"BZZZZZZZZZZZZZZZZZZZZZZZZZZZZZZZZZZZZZZZZZZZZZZZZZ
ZZZZZZZZZZZZZZZZZZZZZZZZZZZZZZZZZZZZZZZZZZZZZZZZZZ
ZZZZZZZZZZZZZZZZZZZZZZZZZZZZZZZZZZZZZZZZZZZZZZZZZZ!"

The very loud buzzer stuck.

I had nowhere to go. The audience was laughing. Becky and Martha were covering their faces. Even the host had to hold back the laughter.

A rock digging place? You've got to be kidding.

"I'm sorry. The correct answer was 'quarry.'"

If we lost this match, I imagined I would be jumping to my death in the quarry next to Becky's house. I was past feeling sick. I was in Kiddie Hell.

Six to five in favor of us and no thanks to me. Neither Martha nor Becky would look at me. If the other team answered the final question correctly, there would be a playoff. I knew I couldn't handle a playoff—I would come completely unglued.

The last contestant was asked to name the nine planets. She looked confident. She quickly rattled off seven planets and when she got to Pluto, she said, "Goofy." I guess she knew it was a Disney character. In the process, she missed Earth completely. I guess some things are too obvious—like four sticks of butter.

We won the match and our parents made us feel like a million dollars. No one even remembered I blew two out of three questions. Except me. I'll never forget it.

We came back the next week and were handily beaten by a superior team. We all missed questions and were just glad to be done. But for two short weeks we were celebrities. We had battled the *Kiddie College* and impressed our friends and family.

I think it was too much pressure for a third grader. It makes me wonder what it must be like to compete in the Olympics or in a national spelling bee. While those people always look so serious, they are excellent at what they do. The excellence comes first.

I was trying to be serious but never thought about being excellent. I might have been much better prepared had I studied. And you know what else? No one ever said, "Just have fun."

*   *   *   *   *

Can you see now that being excellent is what earns us the right to have fun? Did you buy into the myth that to be taken seriously, you had to be serious? Could you resolve, from now on, to be good at what you do while having a good time? Good work and a good time. That's the definition of a rich and balanced life.

The Lights Are On...

Good sense is a thing all need,
few have, and none think they lack.

– Anon

Have you ever been driving down the road and realize you don't remember the past few miles? One of my grad school professors said when this happens; we have actually slipped into a light hypnotic trance. The cool thing is our subconscious is still awake and protecting us from running off the road.

Some people seem to go through life like that, happily living in a trance, unaware of the past few miles. This describes a college classmate and one of my wife's former housemates. Her name is Betty. That may or may not be her real name. I'll let you determine what you would like it to be. She said it was OK if I mentioned her but after reading this you may wonder if she remembers she said it was OK.

Betty is brilliant and beautiful. That's a combination of traits that makes me very uncomfortable even though my wife is also brilliant and beautiful. Don't think I'm just saying that because my wife might actually read this—it's true....dear. I think the thing that makes brilliant, beautiful people intimidating to me is I don't have anything over them. If someone was smart but ugly, at least I could rest easy knowing I'm reasonably good looking. And if someone is beautiful and not smart, I would feel confident that I always get *Far Side* cartoons. But brilliant and beautiful means the only hope I have is a flaw in their common sense. Enter Betty.

Betty received a Bachelor of Science degree in Engineering from the University of Virginia. She turned heads whenever she entered a room. She was fun to be around. And she might actually believe in Santa Claus. Among our friends, Betty stories live large in our college folklore like Grillswiths and One-Eyed Bacon Cheeseburgers (two infamous late-night survival foods). This is her story.

Betty grew up in a suburban setting and had a very normal life. She came to college and immediately made friends with those in our dorm. During her second year, Betty's parents gave her their old Cadillac. It was one of those old long cars that had different zip codes in the front and back. Since many of us did not have "wheels," much less large ones, Betty became our chauffeur whenever we had more than 15 people who needed a ride. We'd load the tank, put the girls up front, the boys in the back and we'd be off for a night of partying.

You can probably guess that parallel parking was not in Betty's skill set. Top that off with a car that resembled an aircraft carrier, and you can easily see that maneuvering the car made for an interesting experience. Every time Betty tried to parallel park, one of us would hang our hand out the window and slap the side of the car as if she had run into the car, the curb or a small animal. Betty would scream, slam on the brakes and yell, "Oh no, what'd I hit?!" OK, admit it, that's funny. But here's the kicker. We could do this two or three times in an evening and she would fall for it every time!

I know, you're skeptical. But read on.

After we graduated, I went to visit Betty in Baltimore. I was speaking at a conference there and she agreed to let me stay with her to save on hotel costs. My wife was going to join me on the second day of the conference. The first night I was there, Betty and her fiancé, Tom, wanted to take me out to their "favorite restaurant." I was excited to see a bit of Baltimore and looked forward to this meal, which they had promised would be fantastic. We rode around for an hour-and-a-half while they tried to find the place. Remember, it was their favorite restaurant! Finally, our stomachs were screaming for some morsel of food, so they gave up and decided to go somewhere else. On the way to somewhere else, we PASSED THEIR FAVORITE PLACE! Still skeptical? Read on.

The level of "legend" given to Betty stories was achieved in an experience that happened around the same time as the restaurant incident. Betty and Tom decided to go away for the weekend to do some white water rafting. Not wanting to leave their beloved cat Little Kitty alone for that long, they decided to take her with them. Now, I know a lot of you may be pet parents and many of you take your animals on vacations and weekend outings so your furry friends don't feel left out. I'd like to remind you that they are animals. They actually enjoy having time on their own and don't need to be carted around like humans. Give them a sunny spot on the floor and they're happy. They're not sitting in the kennel struggling with abandonment issues while you're on vacation. Basically, they're more concerned with the cute Shih Tzu in cage three.

Betty and Tom felt Little Kitty would be lonely without them on their weekend trip so not only did they take her with them; they took her on the raft. In case you haven't pictured this yet, this is Class III white water rapids! (While Class III water may be classified as "intermediate," it still packs a wallop!) And they took a cat on a raft. What do cats fear most? WATER, for gosh sakes!

They were in the water for about 30 minutes when they came to their first stop. The raft was guided up on shore and like a cat out of water, Little Kitty said, "Adios" and was never seen again.

I know this is sad, and we consoled Betty when she shared this with us at a reunion of college friends. Then, as if on cue, we looked at her and said, "WHAT WERE YOU THINKING!?"

Betty realized cats and rafting don't necessarily go hand in hand. She felt awful about the whole experience. Turns out, she and Tom went back the next week looking for Little Kitty......IN A HELICOPTER! If we didn't love her, we'd kill her.

Twenty years after we graduated from college we saw Betty and Tom at a wedding. It was great seeing them and reminiscing about all of the fun we had in college. Betty did not remember all the "Betty stories" but she didn't deny them either. We were blessed with one more story at the wedding.

Apparently, Betty recently hired someone to clean her house. That's not such a big deal. She has two kids and they can afford it. Many of our friends have a cleaning person. But there is one significant difference. Since Betty was having such a hard time getting prepared for the cleaning person, she hired someone else to come in the day before the cleaning person to "straighten up"!

Betty is still beautiful and brilliant and we love her. Whereas she might not have the best common sense, she does have a sense of humor about herself. And that's the saving grace.

*   *   *   *   *

Do you know someone like Betty? Do you find their quirks or eccentricities endearing? One of the biggest lessons I've learned about humor is if we can laugh at our human foibles, others often choose to laugh with us instead of at us. Could you choose to see your own idiosyncrasies as a personality imperfection instead of a personality flaw? By choosing to see it humorously, others will do the same.

Humor Is a
Religious Experience

*A keen sense of humor helps to overlook the
unbecoming, understand the unconventional,
tolerate the unpleasant, overcome the
unexpected and outlast the unbearable.*

– Billy Graham, evangelist

I think God has a sense of humor.

I was raised a Methodist, but am now a Presbyterian. In essence, I've switched teams. Being a Christian is like getting ice cream at Baskin Robbins. It's all ice cream but there are lots of different flavors. I guess over time, some people didn't like the way others organized their religion. So, they just created another one. When I became a Presbyterian, it wasn't because I was unhappy with the Methodists; we just landed in a wonderful Presbyterian church and immediately felt at home.

Now, there is one thing about the Methodists that's a bit annoying. They have this process in which they rotate their ministers every four or five years. By the time I was eighteen, it seemed like our church had gone through 30 or 40 ministers. I guess that's a bit of an exaggeration but it's like some sermons— it may have only been 20 minutes long but you realize you've checked your calendar several times before it was over—it felt like more than it was.

I wonder if the Methodists think you must rotate pastors like tires. Maybe they think it protects churches from getting worn around the edges. Whatever the reason, I think it makes the spiritual journey a little tougher when your tour guide keeps changing.

My wife Wendy and I started looking for a church home when we moved to Reston, Virginia in the mid 1980's. We found Vienna Presbyterian Church about 20 minutes from our home. We had hoped to find one closer to home but were not pleased with the options.

We visited one church and the pastor was asking the congregation to pray that they wouldn't go bankrupt. There's something about that kind of sermon that's not very inviting to visitors. We weren't really looking for a *fixer upper* church.

At another church, we had misread the sign and didn't realize it was a more conservative congregation than we had been accustomed to. Within the first few minutes of the service, the pastor was screaming at everyone to join in a protest march against abortion. I should explain that I'm not pro-abortion, but I'm also not much for marching against it. It's not that I'm wishy-washy; it's that I tend to differentiate between my personal values and others' values. I guess that makes me Pro-Life by Choice.

The last church we visited met in the *cafetorium* of an elementary school. I have nothing against smaller churches who can't afford a building of their own, but I just had a hard time focusing on the sermon when just to the right of the "pulpit" was the pyramid of the five food groups and a large yellow squash that said, "You are what you eat." It made me wonder if the pastor wore a hair net when he served communion.

Now that I'm Presbyterian, I'm not really sure how the Presbyterians and the Methodists differ. I know Presbyterians believe in a concept called predestination. In a nutshell, predestination means God has everything already figured out. So, my previous sentence was already decided before I ever wrote it down. And so was that one. Well, you get the point. Since I am not a theologian and I have never been an expert in religion, please do not write me to complain about my simplistic understanding of predestination. I am pleasantly content to live, as pop artist Andy Warhol said, "as a deeply superficial individual."

Even though I have been an Elder and a Deacon in my church, those positions are more about running the church than knowing the theology. I am often just as confused as the next guy about my faith. I do not know a lot about other religions either. In my small hometown of Emory, Virginia, I was not exposed to a diversity of religions. In Emory, diversity was pretty much captured in Baptists, Methodists, Blacks and Whites. That was about it.

As the years went on, I gradually became more familiar with other faiths. I sat in awe at my first Catholic wedding. One of my fraternity brothers was getting married. The priest administered the Eucharist to the bride and groom and then right there in front of God and everybody, he chugged the rest of the wine. I high-five'd the guy next to me. As a poor alcohol-deprived kid from Appalachia, I remember thinking the priest was pretty cool.

By the time I got to my cousin-in-law's wedding, I was a bit more Catholic savvy. I knew we had to kneel and sit, sit and kneel, and then kneel again. I knew much of the service would be in Latin and even though I had four years of Spanish classes under my belt, it was still undecipherable to me. Come to think of it, if the sermon was in Spanish, I would only recognize the "si's" and "no's."

I also knew when it came time for the Eucharist, the time in the service when Catholics go forward to receive "communion," I was not allowed to participate. Even though I'm Christian, I can't partake of the Catholic's communion. It was home court advantage and I was the visiting team. You would think since we both had the same coach, we could play together, but their rules were different than ours. I knew that, and with the assistance of my therapist, I have accepted it.

When the time came for the communion, our family knew the routine. The ushers would come to our row and give us the *It's-your-turn* nod. In response, we would give the usher the *We-can't-participate-because-we're-Presbyterians* look. The usher would understand and after a brief *Thank you anyway* wink, he would move on. Sure enough, at this wedding, we went through the same routine.

A nod from the usher. A look from us. A wink from the usher. But wait. Something was amiss. My brother-in-law Kyle, who was seated at the end of the pew, was standing up and it only took a moment to realize what was happening. Kyle didn't know the rules. He thought he was supposed to get up and get in the Eucharist line. Heaven help us and Mother Mary too!

Kyle got in line behind a family with eight children. He kept looking forward as he inched his way towards the altar. He had no idea that no one else in our family had gotten up with him. I must admit at this point, it was mildly amusing and getting better by the minute.

Then it happened. Right there in the middle of Saint Somebody's Catholic Church, Kyle turned to say something to one of us behind him. Problem was, none of *us* was behind him. Instead, the next person in line was a member of someone else's family. Kyle looked at them and then his eyes darted back to our row where he saw he had been the only member of the family to get up. The look on his face was that of a condemned man. He knew there was no turning back. It's not like he could have said, "Oh, I forgot I wasn't Catholic and need to go back." He could have faked a heart attack, but surely there would have been a doctor in the house who would have figured him out. So, he was stuck. He was alone and on his way to the altar like Judas at the last supper—an imposter.

That's when I lost it. I lost it in a big way. Had I been drinking the communion wine, it would have come out my nose like milk.

At first, I tried to conceal it. I looked down at the ground, I looked away from Kyle, I even tried to think of something sad—like the fact that Kyle was going to hell for faking Catholicism. But I couldn't hold it in. What started as a snicker developed into a chuckle and led to a laugh. But this was no ordinary laugh. This was forbidden laughter. You're not supposed to laugh in church. You could get struck by lightening or worse yet, "die before you wake." Every attempt to hold in the laughter led to violent spasms throughout my entire body.

My wife was next to me and kept elbowing me.

"Calm down. Stop laughing," she said.

I glanced down the row. Heads were bobbing because I was shaking the pew. Like lighter fluid on a fire, the image of my mother-in-law bouncing on her seat fed my laughter.

Finally, my wife looked at me, pointed toward the exit.

"Leave," she demanded.

How could this be? I was being punished. I had to leave the party. I was being sent to "time out." At this point, I wasn't sure if I'd ever stop laughing, so I begrudgingly obliged and made my way to the back of the church and out into the parking lot.

I've often wondered what the friends of the bride thought as I made my way out of there with tears in my eyes. I bet they thought I had been overcome with emotion and had to leave. That's even funnier. Little did they know I was not some sensitive guy crying at a wedding but just a goof laughing at his brother-in-law. It's no wonder the Catholics don't let us participate in the communion.

I got to the parking lot and realized I had been there before. At previous weddings and funerals, I had taken our children here when they had reached their limit of quiet time. Now, however, I was in the parking lot. I was alone, and I was laughing. Needless to say, the image of this made me laugh even harder. If laughter is the best medicine, I had been inoculated for a lifetime.

Finally, I tried to calm myself down by thinking of some tragedy befalling my family. As I regained composure, I started back to the wedding. Every few steps, I would experience an aftershock. It would start with a small rumble inside and then the corners of my mouth would turn, coupled with short bursts of the giggles. As the contractions became fewer and farther apart, I was able to make my way back to the family pew.

As I returned to my designated seat, Kyle was just getting back from his conversion experience. He had this strange look on his face. It was the same expression I saw on Tonya Harding's face—the *I didn't do anything wrong* look. Kyle tried to pretend as if he *meant* to go up to the altar. But between the crumb of communion wafer on his chin the fact that he knew we knew he couldn't pull it off, he was just plain guilty.

Then the unthinkable happened. Just as Kyle sat down, my sister-in-law Sande turned to me and said, "Wow, he must have been *hungry*."

This time, I just waited in the parking lot until the wedding was over. I was exhausted.

*　*　*　*　*

Do you think it's sacrilegious to laugh in church? Please understand that we can have faith and fun at the same time. Humor is a gift from God and the Bible even instructs us to be joy-full. Therefore humor *is* a religious experience that can bring joy to our lives and others. Our faith should never put us in religious prison but instead should be the reprieve we need from the adversities and adversaries in our world. Maybe we should pray *and* play a bit more often. God help us if we do.

PART II

HUMOR ADDS BALANCE TO THE STRESS IN LIFE

Humor, Cancer, ALS and Death

Analyzing humor is like dissecting a frog.
Few people are interested and the frog dies of it.

– E. B. White, author

Whereas I understand the risk in delving too much into the how's and why's of humor, I have also learned it's important to understand the ways it helps.

I'm convinced a laugh or two a day keeps the doctor away. I'm sure it works as well as an apple and it's a lot more fun.

Much research has been done exploring the connection between laughter and health. Studies show that with laughter, we enhance our immune system, raise our pain threshold, recover from illnesses quicker, we are less susceptible to illnesses recurring and our body gets an aerobic workout. Considering that laughing is an activity most of us thoroughly enjoy, this research is like learning *that chocolate cures cancer*.

Humor balances the negative effects of pain. It also balances the burden of adversity by giving us a break from the ongoing barrage of stress in our lives. Let me give you a few examples in which humor was just what the doctor ordered.

Mr. Smith

One day, while in my role as a hospice social worker, I visited Mr. John Doe Smith (not his real name!). I walked into his bedroom and asked my typical introductory question. "How are you feeling today?" As a trained counseling professional, this was not a particularly pithy opening line. Yet, in the world of hospice care, there were not a lot of choices. It's all relative, and a common question like "How are you doing?" is not quite effective because in general, the patients are not doing well. They're dying. At the same time, they don't want to always be treated as "die-ers." So, asking how someone felt on that particular day puts the question in perspective without saying, "Are you any closer to death?"

Mr. Smith responded to my question by saying, "I feel like I have one foot in the grave and the other on a banana peel."

As a hospice patient, the fact that Mr. Smith just made a humorous reference to death was very uncommon. In fact, it was so uncommon, I was sure it was not intended to be humorous. Risking a blatant misinterpretation, I said, "That's funny."

"I know," Mr. Smith replied as I breathed a sigh of relief. "I used to be the jokester in my family. I shared jokes at dinner, brought home funny movies and looked for any opportunity to have fun. Now that I'm sick, my family treats me as if I'm already dead."

Imagine that. A man facing his own death has the desire and ability to share humor with others yet the people around him are not allowing it to happen. Isn't it amazing how we treat one another? In the name of respect, maturity or reverence, we sometimes miss a wonderful opportunity for connection and balance.

Mr. Smith and I had a long talk about his life, his humor and his illness. It seemed humor was a vital part of his personality and made him the life of the family, so to speak. His banter and perspective were a healthy break from their day-to-day existence, and he brightened their lives with his wit and liveliness. Once he became ill, however, everything changed. His family could not bear to see their strength wilt away. And the way they expressed their grief was through the distance of seriousness. In essence, they could no longer find the fun in their lives.

I asked Mr. Smith if he would allow me to convene a family meeting in which he and I would explain his predicament to the other members of his family. He reluctantly agreed but feared it would further distance him from them.

I asked the family to join us around Mr. Smith's bed. I explained that we had discussed his wonderful sense of humor and how he used to delight the family with his antics. They all smiled and fondly recalled those times.

I asked if things were the same. Hesitantly, his son spoke up and explained they were not. Mr. Smith expressed his regret for this change and said he longed for a time when they could once again laugh together. Not realizing the effect it had on him, his family agreed to recapture the fun between them. The meeting was a cathartic and healing process.

I later learned that after I left that day, Mr. Smith's daughter went to the video store and rented five comedy movies. They planned to watch them all and then sit around and tell jokes. From that point on, humor was going to be a part of Mr. Smith's life…and death.

I saw Mr. Smith a few weeks later and although his illness had progressed, he looked like a million dollars. His family had given back his soul.

Mr. Jones

Mr. Jones had ALS. He was also a simply delightful person.

ALS (Amyotrophic Lateral Sclerosis also known as Lou Gehrig's Disease) attacks the neurons that control the voluntary muscles. What starts with weakness and difficulty moving, the person with advanced ALS becomes totally immobile and unable to communicate. Yet, the brain functions are preserved. Since the eyelids are usually one of the last body parts affected, they become the main form of communication.

Mr. Jones and I shared two important similarities: We both loved cold Coca-Cola over ice and we loved to laugh. Each time I visited him, I was treated to both. There was nothing better than sitting with him, drinking a Coke and watching him laugh. His smile was magnetic and his heart was huge. But over time, his illness progressed to the point he was only able to move his eyelids.

He was unable to interact like he used to, yet he wanted to be included in every activity around him.

On one visit, his wife and I were talking as we sat on separate corners of his bed. We discussed a number of things, including a trip they had taken to Mexico when they were younger. All of the sudden, Mr. Jones' eyelids started fluttering. His wife knew he needed something so she began their routine of using the alphabet to communicate. One blink for yes. Two blinks for no.

"A through M?" she inquired.

One blink.

She began to list them out, "A, B."

One blink. It was "B."

She kept going, "A through M?"

One blink.

"A, B, C, D, E, F."

One blink. Now it was "B, F."

Typically, they had developed a shorthand method of communicating. Spelling every word would take forever, so they decided to abbreviate. She knew "P" meant pee and "BM" mcant, well, BM. "RD" meant radio and "LT" meant light. It was a very efficient yet still a tedious process.

"BF?" she asked. One blink. So, the letters were correct but she couldn't figure out what they meant.

"Do you need to have a BM?" she asked.

Two blinks. No.

"Do you want me to read a book?"

Two blinks.

"Are you bothered by something?"

Two blinks.

This wasn't as easy as she had anticipated. She couldn't figure out what he wanted so after numerous attempts, she knew he would have to spell it out completely.

Over the next five minutes, he spelled, "B, U, L, F, I, T, N, G."

"Bullfighting!" she yelled. "It's bullfighting!"

His eyes fluttered and you could see the beautiful glimmer indicating success.

His wife smiled with a tender look of recognition. Meanwhile, she could see the deep confusions in my eyes.

"He loved the bullfighting on our trip to Mexico."

Amazing.

Here was a man who would take hours to have a normal conversation and I'm sure he was often left out because of the effort. Yet, he was still engaged and wanted to participate. As his wife discussed their trip to Mexico, he wanted us to know he thoroughly enjoyed the bullfighting. We all laughed when we realized what he was trying to say. And even though we did not see a smile, we *knew* there was laughter in his heart.

The Nun

Being a professional speaker allows me the opportunity to work with people I would otherwise never experience. I've spoken to people at NASA, the US Senate, Kellogg's, Ronald McDonald Charities, the Australian Embassy and the Smithsonian. These are cool places to work. Had I not been a speaker, I may have never been given the chance to work with these wonderful organizations.

One of my most memorable experiences was doing a morning workshop for nuns in the Benedictine Order. My friend Sister Catherine had asked if I would help with the retreat for the Sub Prioresses (the "vice presidents" of their respective convent) from all over the country. It was a unique opportunity that was not lost on me.

Most organizations create retreats that actually make you want to—retreat that is. They take their staff to a beautiful location at a beach resort or mountain getaway and then they work them for 10-12 hours a day. It's worse than being at work.

The nuns however, did it right. Their retreat was held in rural Delaware for three days. The first day was educational and included my presentation. The second day was spiritual and included meditation, worship and prayer. The third day was set aside just for fun so they loaded up the bus and went to the beach! I'm sure they avoided getting burned by using nunblock (sorry).

One of the nuns at my workshop shared how a friend, also a nun, had coped with her cancer treatment. When she was going through radiation and chemotherapy, she had been hospitalized and was very weak. Yet her family and friends wanted to check up on her. Because of the many calls she received, she set up a system for taking the calls. She let everyone know she would only take calls from people who would start their conversation out with a joke. In other words, make her laugh and you could talk to her. Don't and you're out of luck!

This "fun nun" knew that humor could sustain her when her physical body had given out. By creating a humor rule, she was able to balance the stress of her disease.

*   *   *   *   *

Are you dealing with a crisis in your life? Are you under stress because you or a loved one is ill? Are you overdue for some *humorelief*? Can you accept that laughing momentarily at something that is funny isn't rude, but therapeutic? Could you, like Mr. Smith, Mr. Jones, and the fun nun choose to look for laughs in an otherwise tough situation? When we are confined to the frailties of our bodies, humor can be a welcome release and respite from the tension and pain. It could be just what the doctor ordered.

A Proper Burial

See everything, overlook a great deal.
– Pope John Paul XXIII

A recent study said something like 53 million Americans have trouble sleeping at night. I've never had trouble sleeping. I can sleep just about any time, anywhere. I sleep on planes, in cars, even at work. But apparently lots of people do have trouble sleeping. I think one reason is they think too much about their stress. I, on the other hand, take the approach that if I'm asleep, I can't think about stress. In fact, I can't think about anything. It may be avoidance or some form of denial, but to me, sleep is a peaceful escape from the many stresses of the world. Humor can also be just the escape you need.

Humor neutralizes the stress we experience. We can't eliminate stress. Life doesn't work like that. Johnny Carson said, "If life was fair, Elvis would be alive and all the impersonators would be dead." Since life isn't fair and we are certain to face the unfairness of stress, we need tools to help us wade through the stressful muck of our lives.

A cool tool is humor. The key is seeing that humor serves as that tool.

In 1997, the Culberson family decided it was time to move to a new house. Ryan, our second child was three and Caitlin was six. The house we were living in was just not configured the way we wanted. It had a tiny master bathroom, which we affectionately referred to as the closet. My office was in the basement so I couldn't hear the UPS man when he delivered a package. And we only had a one-car garage. These were minor problems, but we felt we needed a change. So we put our house on the market and began looking for something else.

About two months into the process, we found our dream house. It had a bright family room with a vaulted ceiling, a two-car garage, an office on the first floor and a master bedroom and bath that could accommodate about 100 average sized adults.

Now, we are not risk-takers. We would have never put a contract on a new house without first selling the old house. But we were afraid we would lose the new house. So we went for it knowing that when we sold our old house, we were assured of making a nice profit. The problem was, real estate was moving slowly and our house had been on the market for two months with only one prospective buyer having seen it. We suspected she was a spy for one of our neighbors who wanted to know our asking price. So we crossed our fingers and every day hoped someone would be interested.

While this whole house-juggling thing was going on, I was serving as a Deacon in my church. One of my Deacon duties was to visit church members who could not get to church on a regular basis. One day I was visiting one of these members, a wonderful woman named JoAnn. I explained our dilemma with the house.

"Have you tried a St. Joseph's?" she asked.

As mentioned before, I'm Presbyterian now but was raised Methodist. I don't know nothin' 'bout no saints. In fact, growing up in Southwest Virginia, the only saint I ever heard about was when my neighbor Charlie would look at a piece of mis-delivered mail and say, "'saint mine."

"What are you talking about?" I said to JoAnn.

She explained the superstition which is shared by realtors (and Catholics, I suppose) that says if you bury a little plastic statue of St. Joseph, you will sell your house. At this point, I feel like I'm negotiating some voodoo ritual and I'll be struck by lightening at any minute. JoAnn reassured me it was OK and then retrieved the very St. Joseph statue she used to sell her house a few years earlier. She gave it to me.

"Try mine—it can't hurt."

I wasn't so sure. I asked my pastor if I was going to get into trouble doing this. He told me not to worry, and pointed out that if I could put my faith in a realtor, I should be able to put my faith in St. Joseph. *Good point.*

That night, I discussed the whole idea with Wendy and she said, "What do we have to lose?"

The next day, I snuck into the front yard about five in the morning, quickly buried the statue and then ran back inside. All day long, I kept feeling like I was playing with forces far greater than me, and I would be taught some major life lesson that might include losing a limb or temporarily losing my sight. Luckily, nothing happened...yet.

Exactly one week later, our house sold. I can't explain it and I don't want to try. I was ecstatic and wanted to give JoAnn a great big hug. At the same time, I was very intimidated by this little statue and didn't really want to touch it. But, I *did* dig it up, wash it off and take it back to JoAnn. When I walked into her room, she had this "I told you so" look on her face. It was getting spookier by the minute.

Two months later, we signed all the papers and moved into our new place without a single problem. The first weekend in our new house, I was eager to work in the yard. I mowed, trimmed bushes and put down several thousand pounds of mulch. I was near the front door spreading one batch of mulch when my rake struck something hard. As I dug into the mulch a little bit more, you'll never believe what I found.

Go ahead, guess.

No really—guess. You won't believe it.

The remains of a human body. Not really, but wouldn't that have made a great story?

There, buried in the yard of my new house was a St. Joseph statue identical to the one we used. How ironic. I guess you could say we had been *sainted*!

Wendy and I had a good laugh about this and told everyone we knew. About two months later, my sister told me about a letter featured in that month's *Reader's Digest*. A man wanted to sell his house and had been told about the superstition surrounding the St. Joseph's statue, so he planted one in his yard. He wasn't sure how he was supposed to bury it so he kept moving it around to different places on their property hoping their luck would change. Finally after several months with no sale, he threw it away in the trash that was picked up and taken to the town landfill. A few weeks later, he read in the local paper that the town had sold the landfill! Go figure.

In the midst of the stress related to a home that wouldn't sell, a move from one house to another and getting everything settled in a new location, St. Joseph popped up to give us a bit of humor. I don't think St. Joseph is the Patron Saint of Humor. At the same time, we were "saved" from the debilitating effects of stress by the buffering effects of humor. Humor can be an accidental or a purposeful tool that won't keep us up at night.

* * * * *

Isn't one of the goals in life to successfully manage stress? When stress is keeping you awake, can you see the humor that could provide a much needed rest from the adversity? Look around you for the humor that will keep you from being buried by too much stress. Allow the humor to dig you out of your funk so you can tackle the challenges you face. You'll soon realize giving into the stress just *'saint* worth it!

This Too Will Pass

Humor does not diminish pain.
It makes the space around it get bigger.
– Allen Klein, author

Sometimes humor sneaks up on us and if we don't enjoy it, we miss what it has to offer.

Isn't it funny how our dreams blend with reality? The phone in our dream is really our alarm clock. The wolf that's chasing us is really the neighbor's dog barking. The cup of water we spill on our lap is, well, you get the picture. Whatever the connection, it usually takes a few minutes to clear our mind and figure out what the reality is.

Early in my 25th year, I woke up about five o'clock in the morning while having a dream that someone was hitting me in the side. When I finally woke up, my side was killing me. I went to the bathroom and immediately got my first clue that something was dreadfully wrong. My urine had turned brown. I don't mean to be graphic but when you're dealing with medical problems, there are certain key clinical indicators that must be described. I had worked in a hospital for several years and even though I was not a trained medical professional, I knew certain things were abnormal. Brown urine was one of them. No amount of black coffee, strong tea or Guinness Stout beer will turn your urine brown. Brown urine is a sign of trouble. The urine and the pain led me to only one conclusion— kidney stone.

I'm sure you've heard the comparison between the pain of having a kidney stone and having a baby. I'm here to de-myth-defy that belief because the pain of a kidney stone feels nothing like that. In fact, the pain of a kidney stone feels more like being pummeled repeatedly in the side by several 300-pound, mentally unbalanced members of the World Wrestling Federation who are trying desperately to prove they really are athletes and not just good actors. It's NOTHING like having a baby. But back to my stone.

You may wonder how I knew brown urine and pain meant I had a kidney stone. My father had suffered with one for nine painful days about a year or so before (more about that saga later). So I knew all the symptoms. I knew the pain I was experiencing was caused by a very small but deadly piece of natural shrapnel that was blocking my internal plumbing. I found out later it was caught in the ureter, the tube connecting the kidney to the bladder. Apparently, our Maker equipped the ureter with an abundance of nerve endings so even the smallest piece of a kidney stone lodged in there feels like a meteor. I remind you that it's not like having a baby.

Luckily, my friend Mike worked at Fairfax Hospital as a pharmacist. Fairfax Hospital was about two miles away and I knew Mike would be going to work soon. So I called him and in between grunts and gasps, I said, "I think....I have....a....kidney stone." A bead of sweat dropped onto the phone cord.

He said he would be right there so I carefully dressed, making sure not to bend the wrong way. As I waited for him, the second hand on the clock ticked away at about one-third its normal speed. About 20 minutes later (according to the clock, but I'm quite sure it had been at least an hour), Mike pulled up to my townhouse. I gingerly slid into his car and quickly discovered up and down motions were not at all pleasant. Then I looked out ahead of the car and realized, for the first time, that there were at least a hundred speed bumps between us and the main road. I wadded up part of my jacket and stuck it into my mouth.

We hit the first bump a bit too fast. The nerves in my ureter informed me they did not like that much. I groaned, hoping Mike would get the hint. We hit the second one even faster. I politely explained to Mike that even though I wanted to get to the hospital as quickly as possible, these speed bumps hurt more than the kidney stone by itself. I had not finished my sentence when we sailed over the third bump. At this point, I grabbed Mike near his ureter and threatened extensive damage if he didn't slow down. We almost didn't have enough speed to make it over the next bump. I wiped the sweat off my lip.

We got to the hospital and Mike helped me waddle into the ER. At this point, the pain was pushing 13 on a 10-point scale. I was instructed to sit at the registration desk where I was met by a friendly, enthusiastic, diligent, very thorough and overly responsible receptionist who needed to "ask a few questions." It was clear she would not let me see a doctor until every single line on the five-page document was completed. The sweat on my lip was beading up again. I gave her *my* medical history, my family's medical history, the story of my father's kidney stone, a brief analysis of the relationships within my family and a rundown of every pill I had in my medicine cabinet. After feeling she had enough to go on, she ushered me into an exam "portal."

The term "emergency room" is quite accurate. There really aren't rooms but simply one big room. They disguise this fact by hanging dozens of curtains which give you a false sense of privacy. Behind each curtain is a gurney, supplies and some equipment. I was instructed to wait on my gurney until the doctor could see me. I glanced around the larger room. There was no one else in there. It then occurred to me that if you are going to need the emergency room, it is a good idea to get there by six in the morning, as I did.

After lying on the gurney for about 15 minutes, I ventured out into the emergentorium to find someone who could give me something to take the edge off the pain. I saw a group of doctors and nurses crowded around a two-way radio.

I said, "Excuse me, could someone give me some pain medicine?"

"We'll be right with you," one of the nurses said. "There is a helicopter on its way and we need to get ready."

As I hobbled back to my gurney, I realized if you're going to have an accident, it's not enough to have it early in the morning. You need to be so bad off you need to be med-evac'd to the hospital to get quick treatment. At this point, the pain was so severe it was starting to ring in my ears. Let me assure you, as I listened to the pain, it did not sound at all like having a baby.

Finally, a doctor came by and began my exam. He asked me the same questions the honor student registrar had asked and he seemed a bit suspicious that I knew I had a kidney stone. I explained, without all of the details, that my father had experienced kidney stones and with the pain and the brown urine, I was pretty sure I had one. He said he would have to do a quick exam and then perform an IVP (Intravenous Pyelogram) to confirm the kidney stone. Whenever I'm in a medical setting, I get so caught up in the lingo, I use my own acronyms. I feel like saying, "AOK; 10-4; EIEIO."

The doctor felt my left side and I yelled. He felt my right side, my back, and my stomach and, no pain. Then he put on a rubber glove and asked me to roll over on my stomach.

Uh-oh.

I had one medical rule during the first 25 years of my life: Do not let a doctor get behind you, especially if he has a glove on. For a quarter of a century I had been successful, but I knew I would not get my pain medicine if I didn't let him complete the examination. Besides, he promised this was the *end* of the exam. Sorry.

The doctor placed his finger in a location where no one else's finger had ever been. And the most amazing part of the experience was when he said, "Do you feel any unusual discomfort?"

At this point, I was trying to pinpoint the sensation I was feeling. In the midst of the unbelievable pain of the kidney stone, I had the distinct feeling his "finger" was actually his entire right arm. I said, "Do you mean the discomfort I'm feeling because your finger is where it shouldn't be?"

He said, "Oh, that's to be expected."

For the first time that day, I laughed out loud. I had expected a shot. I had expected a challenging registration process. I had expected to wait a while in the ER. I had not expected to get a rectal visitation. Then this matter-of-fact doctor made me laugh. And for a moment, the pain disappeared. Just a moment, mind you. After that, it was back in full force.

The rest of the kidney stone experience was somewhat uneventful. I got my shot of Demerol and shortly after the shot, I relaxed so much, I passed the kidney stone into my bladder where it no longer caused me any problems. All in all, I was only in pain for four short hours. Compared to having a baby, that's not too bad. Of course, it's nothing like having a baby.

*   *   *   *   *

Is something causing you pain? Whether it's physical or mental pain, humor can help. Humor may not be able to erase the pain entirely; it can at least mitigate the pain or ease it momentarily. Either is better than suffering with no reprieve in sight.

Shtick the Landing

*If there is a 50-50 chance that something can
go wrong, then nine times out of ten it will.*

– Paul Harvey

Stress can cause us to do somersaults before we even know it. The trick is to realize we are under stress before it gets a hold on us. Sometimes we have to be reminded of that a few…hundred times before it sinks in.

I always considered myself athletic even though my stats did not support my opinion. For instance, I ran track in eighth and ninth grades. My specialty? High hurdles and the high jump. The problem was I was physically low. I was only five feet, three inches tall. I couldn't even have gotten high on drugs.

So here I was competing in events requiring height and jumping ability. Jumping I could do. In fact, I didn't run hurdles, I jumped them. My coach said my form was perfect. I just spent more time in the air than my competitors. The trick to running high hurdles is to keep as much of your stride as possible, as if the hurdles weren't there. At 5'3", the only way I was doing that was to run under them. The leggy fellows' strides were so well coordinated; they would glide over the hurdle and then quickly take three steps before the next one. For me, it was a series of five steps and then a leap, five steps and a leap. Well, you get the picture. Suffice it to say I never won a race.

As for high jumping, I could jump better than most Caucasian boys. I just started lower than they did. And while it is considered an accomplishment to jump one's height, at 5'3" that was only two inches higher than the height at which the competition started. When it was my turn, I would look intensely at the bar while I concentrated on how high it looked. I would hop twice on my right foot and then surge forward, picking up speed as I approached the jumping area just in front of the bar. I would turn my back to the bar, arch my back into perfect Fosbury Flop form and crack my head on the bar. Most guys brushed against the top of the bar. I would knock it off from underneath, which meant it would usually fall on top of me once I landed into the foam pit. It was humbling, to say the least. But I was much more successful at track than at basketball.

Basketball has it all. Speed. Skill. Finesse. And brilliant winter legs protruding from short, silky shorts. If a girl had worn the bottoms to my basketball uniform, she would call them hot pants. But on me, they looked like I had forgotten to put on pants over my boxers. Still, it was a small sacrifice for the sweet smell of success; when with two seconds left on the clock, you put up the game winning shot to the cheers of your parents, homeroom teacher and the puberty-ridden cheerleaders. I really loved the aura of basketball. Problem was, I sucked.

I was short, timid and weak. I was not a star player. In fact, I was a thread. I was not even good enough to be on a string (You know, first string, second string, etc.). In one game, I went up for a lay-up, got fouled, made the foul shot and then stole the ball two more times, all within about one minute. The coach took me out. I have no idea why and I wasn't about to ask. He might tell me I sucked. And at the age of 14, I couldn't handle that.

One day, at the end of my second and last season on Junior Varsity basketball, I snuck a look at my stats. Big mistake. My average playing time was 20 seconds per game. That means my average sitting time was 31 minutes and 40 seconds per game. It's no wonder I couldn't perform once I got in the game. There was way too much pressure.

What's worse, I averaged only .2 points per game! At that level of play, I had to play five games just to score a point. I may have been more patient as a kid than I am today, but that's asking a lot.

So track and basketball didn't work out. Luckily, I was good at tennis and became the number one player in my school for four years in a row. Of course, tennis is not one of the most popular sports in southwest Virginia. In fact, a couple of players on the team used badminton rackets since they didn't have tennis rackets. And they would win. Go figure.

To compensate for my lack of success in sports, I used to develop my own athletic activities. Dave Williams and I were always looking for ways to get a laugh. Two particular techniques worked extremely well.

The first was the Fake a Fall Down the Stairs Trick. I would securely grab the handrail of the stairwell with my left hand and position my upper and lower right arm over the edge of the rail. With the rail under my armpit, I would slide down the rail while my legs flailed wildly as if I had lost all control and was in a free fall. It was quite a sight and was guaranteed to elicit laughs from fellow students and hand-covered gasps from the teachers. We rarely got into trouble though, because it was just clean fun. Dave and I reveled in the notion that we were highly skilled humor technicians.

Another fun generator was the Fake Fight Trick. In between classes, Dave and I would pretend to get into a tussle. It would start with a shove and verbal combat and progress to the point that Dave would place his hand behind my head and shove me toward the bank of metal lockers. I would smack the locker with my hand pretending to hit my face on the locker and then fall back onto the floor holding my forehead. It wasn't until we got older that we discovered this technique was taught in the upper level courses at the World Wrestling Federation Training Camp. We felt honored to share the same techniques with Hulk Hogan and Governor Ventura. It was clear that I was much better at comedy athletics than the real ones.

So when I went to college, I did not pursue formal athletics. I played on intramural teams but never on a real team. I did develop one more valuable comedy athletic skill however—the Horizontal Light Post Trick.

This particular gag was usually unveiled after an evening of bar hopping with my friends at the University of Virginia aka The University or Mr. Jefferson's Academical Village. I would position my left arm against the outside of a light post so that my hand was below my elbow and the inside of my forearm was flat against the post. I would then grab the inside of the post with my right hand so that my fingers pointed downward. It would appear as if I were going to pull the post out of the ground.

Here was the trick: I would position my right elbow against the pointy part of my right hip. By pulling with my left arm and pushing with my right hand, I could raise my entire body to a horizontal position parallel to the ground. I looked like a human pennant, like that insurance company's television ad. It was way cool and most people had no idea how I did it.

Once I got the obligatory "oohs" and "ahs," I would spring from the light post, arch my back and do my best impression of Nadia Comaneci. Such was the life of fame as a comedy athlete.

In 1999, some sixteen years after I graduated *suma cum lately* from The University, my wife, my two children (4 and 7 year olds) and some friends were enjoying dinner together in Washington, DC. After the dinner, we were walking the six blocks back to our cars when I got this great idea.

"Have you ever seen the light post trick?" I asked my friends and their children.

They had not, so I figured it was a great opportunity to wow them with my version of David Copperfield gymnastics. Now please understand I was an out of shape 38-year-old man who had retired from comedy athletics 18 years prior, the same year I had knee surgery and recurring back spasms. But this is the problem with my humor-ness. When the opportunity arises, it takes over and I have little control.

So, I did not hesitate to *mount* the closest light post and slowly (think slowly here and then make it slower) lifted my legs to just shy of parallel to the ground. I could hear muscles screaming for release and I think I actually burst a blood vessel in my forehead. But, I received the customary and much anticipated "oohs and aahs," and then quickly got off that darn light post.

I think it is reasonable to say I did not *shtick* the dismount. I tried to conceal the throbbing pain and burning sensation shooting down the left side of my body as I made my way back to our car. After several minutes of discomfort, I began to feel like *Nausea* Comaneci.

The next morning, our kids woke us up by jumping into bed with us. As I began to come alive, I noticed soreness in the bicep area of my left arm. I raised my shirtsleeve to reveal the nastiest, ugliest, purplest bruise extending from my armpit to my elbow. It was hideous. It looked like I had been in a car accident. And it was really tender. I raised my sleeve and immediately showed it to my wife.

"Look at this awful bruise," I whimpered. "Do you think it's broken?"

My wife rolled her eyes, "I doubt it."

"Do you think I should go to the hospital?"

"I'm sure it will be fine."

As I surveyed the damage, my son and daughter became very interested in dad's new "boo boo." It's curious that children are so obsessed with bodily injuries.

"Let me see," Caitlin said. "How did you get that?"

I promptly showed her the bruise, making sure she didn't touch it lest I'd have to take a Percocet, and said, "I got this bruise when I performed the light post trick last night. I should have never tried it at my age. I wonder if I should call my primary care physician."

My wife ignored me and went in to take a shower.

Caitlin looked at me and then looked at the bruise and declared, "You know dad, it may have hurt, but you impressed *everybody!*"

"That's *my* daughter," I proudly thought.

*   *   *   *   *

Has stress ever knocked you off your feet? Have you ever noticed when you're flat on your back, you can see the stars? Humor can be that spot of brilliance that shines brightly during the darkness of stress. We can't maneuver through life if we allow darkness to consume us. If you can find fun when you're off balance, you are much more likely to shtick the landing.

PART III

HUMOR FORCES YOU TO SEE A NEW PERSPECTIVE

Ryan's New Game

Growing old is mandatory.
Growing up is optional.
– Art Gliner, humorist

One of the greatest benefits of humor is it allows us to see things from a different perspective.

I like details. I love to check something off my "to do" list. The very act is euphoric and somehow gives me a sense that I'm worth something. I've accomplished something great because I have one less detail. In reality, the details don't mean squat. Don't you love the phrase, "don't mean squat"? I have no idea where it came from but the word squat is quite cathartic. It feels good to say it. Squat. Squat. I feel so much better.

I've been called anal retentive—anal for short—because I like order. I believe this comes from my attempt to control external events by putting things in order. It's embarrassing to admit that I love cleaning up clutter but it does make me feel like I've made something better, thus making me feel that I'm better. That's where the anal details come in.

Unfortunately though, life is not about details. Other anal people will try to convince you that it is but in the big scheme of things, it's really about the process.

When my son Ryan was five, he went to a church-based kindergarten called the Ark Academy. The Ark Academy was a small pre-school and kindergarten that had the bow of the Ark sticking out from the side of the building. Wooden giraffes, lions and elephants could be seen rising above the deck. My kids thought it was really cool and I did too.

One day I retrieved Ryan from the playground, buckled him up in the back seat of the car and began the ride home. Ryan was full of energy that day and I could see he had something to say by the way he wriggled and jostled in his car seat.

"How was your day?" I asked.

"Know what?" he replied.

"What?"

With a grin the size of a slice of cantaloupe, he said, "We made up a game today."

"Really? How exciting. Tell me about it."

"Well, it goes like this," he said. "We all went out on the playground and took our shoes off." At this point, he covered his mouth and giggled as if he had gotten away with a kinder-garten felony by taking his shoes off on the playground.

"Then, we ran around the swing set as many times as pos-sible and whoever got around the most number of times, won!" He screamed this last part.

His grin got bigger, if that was even possible.

I was soaking it all in. I could envision the entire scene. My son had gotten his first taste of competition and better yet, his first victory. I was so proud. I imagined his future. It would start with soccer and karate awards. Then he would receive the trophies, the scholarships and maybe even the Nobel Prize. I was certain this was how Albert Einstein would have behaved on his kindergarten playground. My son's future was bright and it was most likely genetic.

As parents, we figure our kids out long before they realize we're onto them. Sometimes we surprise them with our magic knowledge just to maintain the illusion of our wisdom. Other times, we let them figure it out on their own to encourage their own personal development. This was one of those times. I didn't want to ruin what I knew my son had accomplished. So, I played dumb, which my family will gladly attest comes very naturally for me.

"Who won?" I proudly asked.

His smile leapt off his face and was replaced with a confused and disappointed frown.

"I don't *know*."

In his eyes, I had totally missed the point. I'm sure this smart five-year-old was thinking, *it wasn't about winning Daaaaaaad. We invented a game.*

That's it. It was the process. The creation and the implementation. It wasn't about who won. I had just stumbled onto one of the *FUN*-damental differences between children and adults. For adults, so much value lies in the result. Our image, our reputation, our self esteem, our identity all get wrapped up in "Who won?" For kids, it's about the process—if it's not fun, it's not worth doing.

* * * * *

Have you become a *groan* up? Have you lost the ability to see the process because of all the details associated with being an adult? If so, try to see where the child inside you is hiding. Chances are he/she is off somewhere playing. Seeing the humor in every day events can help you find the child you've left behind.

Doorbell Music

We made too many wrong mistakes.
– Yogi Berra, coach

Someone once said, "If you keep doing what you've always done, you'll keep getting what you've always gotten." It's hard to see outside our normal patterns of behavior for new and improved methods of doing things. It's a lot easier to do the same old things, rather than use new brain power to come up with new ideas. I may have a mind for creating humor but I don't always look at problems with a creative perspective.

Growing up, my family was probably considered middle class by the socioeconomic standards in Emory, Virginia. We had more than we needed—decent clothes, good southern fried food on the table and a typical used sedan for a car, but we did not have what might have been referred to as luxury items like a dishwasher, color TV or indoor plumbing. Just kidding, we had indoor plumbing.

I can remember my dad saying things like, "Color means more things can go wrong with the TV. We don't need color," or "If you didn't drink so much Coca-Cola, we'd be driving a Cadillac." He lived through the depression, so if we weren't constantly closing the refrigerator door or cleaning up spills with a napkin instead of paper towel, we were going to end up in the "poor house." I always wondered what the poor house was. I had never seen one but if it had color TV, it might not be so bad.

The other thing we didn't have was a luxury house. It was a modest house that my father bought in the 1940's for $8,625. It was not finished and he did the work to make it livable (notice, I didn't say he finished it). It had a dirt basement, a coal furnace that sometimes backed up, plaster walls, real hardwood floors, and a downright scary attic. Most importantly, it did not have a doorbell. I guess I grew up in the house of hard knocks! Sorry, couldn't resist…again.

My neighbor Mike (coincidentally, the same Mike who helped me with my kidney stones) had a much nicer house than ours. His had wall-to-wall carpeting, a fake gas fireplace with pretend logs, a finished basement, a dishwasher, a color TV and a perfectly tuned doorbell. I loved to visit his house. I'd get him to "turn on" the fireplace while I watched in amazement.

How's it do that? I wondered.

Somewhere along the way, I interpreted these "things" as symbols of status, which unfortunately gave far too much importance to things in my external environment. I think I even measured my sense of self worth by the things we had. If I had things, I was worthy, and if not, somehow I wasn't.

Wendy and I bought our first house in 1986, just after we were married. Wendy had been working at IBM for two years. During the entire time at IBM, she put away the maximum amount she could into savings. She kept her expenses down and made the most of her income. She was shrewd and very smart.

I had been a full-time graduate student for two years. I worked summers and part-time on the weekends while in school. I took out every loan available to me and ran my credit card up to its limit. By the time we got married, I had nothing in the bank, my credit card was at its meager $500 limit and for two months I had worked as a hospice social worker making $18,000 a year. I didn't have squat (doesn't that fit just perfectly here). Wendy agreed to pay off my credit card if I would cut it in half. That was a no-brainer.

So when it came time to buy the house, everything—the cash, the collateral and the security—came from Wendy. I loved this woman!

To me, our house was amazing. It had three bedrooms, two-and-a-half bathrooms, a gigantic concrete basement (status), wall-to-wall carpeting (status), a dishwasher (status), a large master bedroom and of course, a doorbell (big time status). The first night in the house, when we were unloading boxes, I just pushed the doorbell to hear the chimes. It was music to my ears. I imagined how important I was but then I came to my senses and realized Wendy had the status and I had, well, a great sense of humor and the good sense to marry a smart, attractive woman.

One day after we moved into the house, I noticed the doorbell didn't work. Egad. This can't be. That's like having trouble starting the Mercedes or finding a leak in the wall of the pool. My status symbol didn't work! I tightened all the wiring and amazingly, got it working again.

For the next five years, my doorbell worked sporadically at best. I am not a handy person, so I had no idea why this was happening. I tightened and retightened connections and replaced the chimes. Each time I fixed what I thought was the problem, it only worked for a short time. I considered calling someone to fix it, but Wendy thought it was crazy to pay a repairman for a silly doorbell. She clearly did not realize how important this silly doorbell was to me. Still, I had to admit I couldn't justify paying to fix something which could be bypassed by a simple knock on the door. However, the loss of status was depressing.

One night, I asked my brother-in-law Kyle to look at the door-bell for me. I retrieved my toolbox from the basement and the two of us got busy analyzing this perplexing situation. We tightened everything, which I guess is an important male response to inconsistent problems—*must need to be tightened*. Our initial evaluation was that everything was in order. Then came the big test. We pushed the button and the most satisfying sound in the world blared out—a great big DING, DONG. It worked! I wasn't sure what we did but it didn't matter, it worked. We gave each other a high-five, put the tools away and had a beer to celebrate. I could feel my status tank filling back up inside of me. Of course that might have been the beer or a slight case of gas.

A few minutes after Kyle and I fixed the doorbell, I just had to hear that sound again. I went to the door, pushed the button and...nothing. I pushed it again. And again. And again. Still nothing. The dang thing didn't work anymore. My status started to drain so I quickly got my tools out, took chimes apart and assessed the situation. Aha, we missed a loose wire. We tightened it and everything else just for good measure. My hands were shaking. I hesitantly pushed the button. DING, DONG! Glorious. I had no idea what we did, but it didn't matter. High-fives all around and another beer to celebrate. The status tank was once again full.

Later that night, my mind wandered back to the door. A voice told me not to try it but I couldn't control the urge to hear the sound. It was now an addiction. I had to know it worked. I sloshed over to the door and pushed the button........nothing. There was only one explanation. Poltergeist. Satan had taken up residence in my home.

Kyle and I took out the tools, tightened and hammered everything (since *we* were, shouldn't everything else be?). Of course, the doorbell worked. At this point, I was suicidal. I looked at the two ends of the electrical wires and considered sticking them in my mouth. But I figured that probably wouldn't work either.

Kyle and I sat on the couch dumbfounded. We looked at each other in our beer induced stupor and didn't know what to think. As my foggy mind retraced the sequence of events, I began to see a pattern. Doorbell doesn't work—take the tools out—tighten everything—doorbell works—put tools away. Repeat. I went over this several times and then it occurred to me. The doorbell never worked when the tools were put away. Eureka! I must have magic tools!

After several simple tests, our suspicion was confirmed. The idiot who built my house had wired the doorbell to the light in my basement where my tools were stored. In other words, the doorbell only worked when the basement light was on. What *This Old House* episode told the builder to do this? Perhaps they ran out of wire on the way to the fuse box and just hooked it into the light. Or maybe they got the wires mixed up and the garage door opener was supposed to be connected to the basement light. Who knows what they were thinking? All I know is when I had my basement finished; I wired the doorbell to nothing more than electricity. From that point on, I had the ding dong status I had longed for.

*   *   *   *   *

The beauty's supposed to be in the details, right? Well, maybe that's true, but the perspective's in the process. Humor keeps the process in the proper perspective. Are you getting all wrapped around the axle of something that's driving you crazy? Why tighten up, when you can lighten up? Humor is not only music to our ears but poetry to our minds.

Making the Grade

An optimist laughs to forget.
A pessimist forgets to laugh.

– Tom Nansbury

My wife told me I'm more pessimistic than I used to be. I told her to quit bothering me. Not really. In fact, I thanked her for telling me. She opened my eyes to something I didn't realize was happening. I was becoming cynical. It's a reasonable line of thinking since the world is full of crap, people are no good and everything sucks anyway. Nonetheless, I had gotten a bit cranky in my middle age.

I don't mean to put you in the therapist's chair but I believe my cynicism comes from my own fears and insecurities. As long as I can criticize others, I still look good. Once everyone else looks good, my view of myself is in the toilet. It's a never ending battle to balance my view of myself, my view of the world and my reality. So my wife has to intervene every once in a while to keep me sane. How's she doing? Don't answer that.

Wendy and I are very different when it comes to the way we behave yet we are very similar in our core beliefs. We have the same values, the same views of the world and total trust of one another. We are true partners and we love and respect one another. But it wasn't always that way.

First Date?

When I first met Wendy Colclough (pronounced cole-claw) on the balcony of my college dorm, I was immediately infatuated with her. Unfortunately, she did not feel the same way about me. She reminds me that when she met me, I was wearing bibbed overalls with no shirt. OK, so I came from "the country" and that's what we wore—not all the time, just for special occasions.

At lunch a few years ago, a friend of mine asked me what the "bib" in bibbed overalls was. I proudly explained that the bib was the portion of the overalls that covers your chest and is usually equipped with two straps and a pocket. He glibly replied, "Then what are the overalls without bibs called?"

I panicked. No one had ever challenged my mountain heritage so directly. As I thought about it, I realized overalls without bibs are basically jeans. That can't be right. There has to be a better explanation. As perspiration built up on my forehead, I felt myself becoming a hick. I actually thought I felt one of my front teeth loosening. I could see the reflection of a country bumpkin in his eyes.

I said, "If you don't know that, then *I'm* not going to tell you."

He chuckled and returned to his mixed greens salad. I finished my chicken fried steak and felt clueless. I still wake up in the middle of the night wondering what bib-less overalls look like.

Needless to say, Wendy was not impressed with overalls or my bib.

Then, one November night during our freshman year, we went out on a "group date." Group dates are conveniences for college students who don't have steadies. On a group date, no one is romantically connected to anyone else in the group. I should know. I had a lot of group dates in high school and early college.

On that group date in November of 1979, while watching the Skip Castro band at the Mineshaft Bar near the University of Virginia, I reached over and held Wendy's hand. And she held it back! I was all gooshy inside. This must be love. Where I come from, holding hands was serious. For some of us who were less experienced, it was a sign of impending marriage. I was on cloud nine. I had a real date and maybe even a girl-friend.

The next day, my dreams were crushed. Apparently, in New York, where Wendy was from, holding hands meant noth-ing. It was as common as saying "bless you" when someone sneezed. How could this be? The skin on our hands touched. We intertwined our fingers. It was sensual. It was nothing like gesundheit!

She explained that she had a boyfriend at another school and she had no intentions of dating someone here. Our "date" was insignificant to her and I was dropped before I was even picked up.

To make a long story short (ever notice how when people say this, it's already too long?), I ignored Wendy after that. You see, I had been way too infatuated with her. Once I knew the score, I couldn't hang out with her anymore. It would be too painful. So, I used the only method I knew to avoid the discom-fort; I avoided her.

I sat at a different lunch table with other friends. Whenever I came into a room where Wendy and other girls were sitting, I acknowledged everyone else. I never made eye contact or else her brain waves would somehow detect that I had weakened. For several months, I was quite successful. And I was miser-able. Avoiding her did nothing to anesthetize the pain of wanting to be around her.

The following February, our dorm had a Valentine's dance. Once again, a "group" of us headed to the dance. Not expecting to find anyone special, I bobbed and weaved in a group dance with 50 other people to Bruce Springsteen's *Rosalita* and the Who's *Magic Bus*. We were drinking, laughing, singing and dancing. It was a typical college party.

Somehow during the confusion of the alcohol and the groupness, I ended up next to Wendy. Before I could successfully ignore her, she took my hand.

I said, "Bless you."

She didn't get it, but then she hadn't lived in my hell for the past few months.

She said, "Why don't you talk to me anymore?"

I didn't know what to say. I didn't want to be blunt and tell her she had ruined my existence and that I had considered the priesthood. If I admitted how much she meant to me, she would win. Yet I felt like she was giving me an opening that might actually quell the bleeding ulcer I had developed since our pre-dating breakup.

"I liked you so much last fall," I said, "I just couldn't be around you if you didn't like me back."

Now, you have to give me credit. That was a killer line.

She said, "Let's dance."

So we danced. First, we danced fast. Then, we danced slow. I now understand why some Baptists don't like dancing. It felt great and yet I didn't take advantage of the moment. I was afraid of being dumped again. I was the perfect gentleman.

During one of the slow dances, we kissed. Apparently kissing means more than a sneeze in New York.

This is how I met my future wife. The South had risen again and I am still in heaven.

I Scored!

Wendy and I are very different when it comes to how we view the future. I tend to assume everything will be fine unless I find something that proves otherwise. I expect the positive and then deal with the negative if I need to. Part of this is my avoidance of negativity. I figure if I don't think about it, it won't happen.

Wendy, on the other hand, would prefer to assume the worst, on the off-chance things don't turn out like she hopes. That way, she is not disappointed. By expecting the negative, she is pleasantly surprised when it doesn't materialize. This is what I call Reverse Escape Pessimism and by the way, it's incurable.

We discovered this difference early in our courtship at UVA. Wendy was an engineer and I was in liberal arts (whatever that means). In some ways, she was in real college and I was in unemployment training. Not that my classes were easy. I was destroyed by Organic Chemistry and Cell Physiology. But I also took classes in Perception, Abnormal Psychology and The History of Circus in America! I did not have a compelling argument for a Rhodes Scholarship.

Here's how our differences usually played out. Wendy would finish an exam. When I would see her later that day, she would be devastated. She'd mope around, saying over and over, "I know I failed that test." In specific detail, she would describe the questions she missed and how she just knew she could never have passed with those incorrect answers. For the next couple of days, she would live in this un-comfort-able funk, convinced she would flunk out of college and end up working at McDonald's with me. Needless to say, she had higher aspirations.

At UVA, and I assume at most colleges, professors posted the grades on their office doors and we, the victims of their psychological torture, would gather 'round the list like Romans at the gladiator matinee.

Wendy would make her way to the "coliseum" and force herself to look at her score. To her surprise, she not only would have the best grade in the class, but the professor would set the curve based on her grade. In other words, she was the standard by which her classmates were measured. She was the Grand Poobah. The Queen of the Exam. Best in Show. In four years of engineering at the University of Virginia, my lovely Wendy received one A minus. And that was the worst it ever got.

I, on the other hand, had a slightly different experience.

After I took an exam, I was ecstatic not just because the torture was over but because I knew I had done very well. I would proudly sashay back to my dorm with the look of a poker player who has no idea his pair of threes is just not that good. I would announce to my roommates that I had finished my test and in fact had "aced it." I would exchange high fives with everyone in the room and would confidently explain that I knew I had done well because I was the first one to leave! Obviously, you can see the tragedy of my feeble mind.

For several days, I would not only live on Cloud Nine, I would own it. The sky was blue, the birds were singing and I was probably going to be asked to live with the exceptional students on The Lawn during my last year. Confident I would be accepted at Harvard Graduate School or and perhaps given a He's a Jolly Good Fellowship, my troubles were over. I was smart.

Then the moment of truth would arrive. The affirmation that the last minute studying had paid off—that you actually could party too much *and* make good grades. That there was no genetic defect in growing up in Appalachia.

I went to my professor's office to get the final proof of my achievement and to leave the coliseum as Galadiatorus Unum.

I glanced at the list of grades and quickly noticed I was not in the first few on the list. Perhaps he accidentally put my first name last. I looked again. Not there. I kept going down the list. Not there. Not there. As I crouched down near the bottom of my professor's door hoping at this particular moment he did not come rushing out, I noticed my name.

Culberson, Ronald   68   C-

Crushed, I would escape to the local student bar and hope to spend an evening in the supportive reassuring arms of my A+ girlfriend.

Unfortunately, she was studying.

*   *   *   *   *

Is your cynicism and pessimism causing you to fail life's multiple-choice exam? There really are other ways to look at most experiences. Even when the world around us seems to be frowning, we can stand on our heads and it will be smiling. With a bit of humor, we can all score big.

Humor Leaves a Mark

*I learned quickly that when I made
others laugh, they liked me.*

– Art Buchwald, humorist

I used to tell my mother I wouldn't be happy until I was famous. Funny, I still feel that way. I know that may sound vain and shallow, but I've never considered myself a deeply thoughtful person to begin with.

For instance, I love all types of music and I have favorite songs. Yet, I can't tell you the words to most of them. I'm affected by the music-beat-voice combination but the words often escape me. I also miss the symbolism you find in good movies. I love them for their entertainment value, but the underlying message may go right over my head. That doesn't mean there's no substance to me or this book. I just don't understand it if there is.

I have a wonderful wife, beautiful children, and a fantastic life. But deep inside, I have this desire to be famous.

I sometimes imagine what the experience would be like. Paparazzi following me and my family trying to get a candid shot of us doing mortal things. My face on the cover of *Time* and *Newsweek* (ok, maybe *The Star* and *The Enquirer*). Posing for a "Got Milk?" ad. That all seems so cool and yet I know it would be a drag after awhile. Somehow though, it would feel like getting my passport stamped—I'd be approved.

Don't get me wrong. This desire is not so strong that I would rob the local K-Mart just to get my name in the paper. Rather, I want to do something people will fondly remember. Maybe that's it; I need to be remembered. Like most of us, I want to leave a legacy so my life means something to others. It's hard for me to imagine that when I die, I will disappear from people's minds. Perhaps this legacy thing is like the movie *It's a Wonderful Life*. George Bailey didn't realize the way he touched others. Maybe I am leaving a legacy and just don't know it.

Invisible Wrasslin'

My dad has been in Rotary for almost fifty years. Rotary was founded in 1905 by Paul Harris and is one of the largest service organizations in the world. My dad is eighty-five and the oldest Rotarian in his local club. He's almost as old as Rotary and has been involved half as long as it has existed. That's something. With all of the service projects he's participated in, he has definitely left a legacy. In fact, there is a bronze plaque at the entrance to Emory and Henry College acknowledging the many contributions of my father.

I am also a Rotarian. I joined in 2000 and have perfect attendance. That means I have not missed a weekly meeting since I joined. I'm proud of that because it requires a commitment and I'm not the best at commitments. Rotary is fun though, and I enjoy going to meetings and volunteering for service projects. Hundreds of thousands of men and women around the country are bound together by the Rotary motto "Service Above Self."

I visited my dad's club recently. Since I grew up in that community, I know many of the members. Many of the old guys are still around. One of our friends, Neel smiled at me and said, "Ronnie, (my nickname from birth until it was eliminated by the need to mature in college), are you still doing the invisible wrestler?"

"No," I chuckled, "I gave that up years ago."

Only as an adult do I realize how strange that question may seem. You see, when I was a kid and prior to my current level of perceived maturity, I was the class clown in school, church, and wherever a group of potential laughers gathered. I was the wise-cracking guy that teachers hated, yet I had a certain sophistication to my humor that actually endeared many adults to me.

One gag I used to perform was a pretend wrestling match in which I would appear to compete against an invisible wrestler. Television wrestling was in its infancy and as impressionable kids, we loved the athletic antics of Hulk Hogan, Andre the Giant and Rowdy Roddy Piper. So I invented this shtick, which I performed at parties, my youth group meetings, and at band camp.

The key to making this ridiculous pantomime work was to make it look like the invisible wrestler was real. To begin, I would pull what appeared to be a folded piece of plastic out of my pocket. I would carefully unfold it and begin to "inflate" my opponent. As an adult, I now realize inflatable partners are not legal in the county where I grew up but that's another story. Once inflated, I would then pretend to face off with this invisible foe in a knock down, drag out "wrasslin" match. I would attack, only to be thrown about the floor in a series of professional wrestling-esque maneuvers. The success of the gag was that I was getting beat by someone you couldn't see. Remember, I grew up in a town of only 280 people, and many of them were married to their relatives.

After being thrown, flipped and tossed, I finally produced an invisible pin from my pocket and deflated my opponent. The whole event lasted about one minute but it usually generated uproarious laughter and thunderous applause. As is common in a small rural town where the folks don't get enough of the quality entertainment necessary for normal brain development, I was often asked to perform "that thare invisible wrassler thang" whenever a social event got boring. I guess many of the smarter people enjoyed it because they couldn't believe I would go to such lengths just to get a laugh. Therein lies the beauty — it was easy for me and quite memorable. It left a mark on the brains of my friends and family.

Twenty six years later, Neel still remembered my invisible wrestler. My family doesn't even remember my finishing second in the county tennis tournament, receiving my college fraternity's highest award, or my becoming a manager after only three years into my career. But when Neel mentioned the invisible wrestler, my dad remembered.

Funny how humor does that.

Frolicking Rotarians

The scene was not suitable for the event. The Barter Theater was the State Theater of Virginia. It was one of the oldest theaters in the country. During the depression, actors gave performances in exchange for food and livestock. That's how The Barter Theater got its name. But the Rotary Frolics was lacking in talent and was not the caliber of entertainment for a dignified theater.

Every year, the Rotary Club in Abingdon put on a talent show at The Barter Theater. At one time in its history, it included some of the best local talent — bluegrass bands, singers, dancers and storytellers. But as time went on, the talent was replaced by Rotarians who performed skits, impersonations, jokes and worst of all, songs. It was horrible. The worse it got, the more the public loved it. Year after year, they sold out the 800-seat theater with three repeat performances, making more than $15,000 for local charities.

My dad emceed this event for forty years. I dreamed of being in the Rotary Frolics because I believed it would make me famous. I figured they could use me to balance out the bad acts, especially the magician who locked himself in a trunk and couldn't get out. I had no idea what I could do. The local talent was usually a band, dancer or singer. I didn't play in a jazz band and I couldn't dance or sing. All I had was a quick wit and an invisible wrestler. Best I could tell, I was not Frolics material. That's got to be the worst.

Then came the call. Ed Damer, the director of the Frolics, called me in the fall of my senior year in high school.

"Ronnie, we thought you might be able to do some comedy in the Frolics this year," he said.

I was transported to the blinding glare of the spotlight. I saw myself wearing a tuxedo and one of those long white scarves. I signed autographs and did television appearances. I imagined saying, "It all started at the Rotary Frolics."

"Ronnie? Ronnie?"

"I'd love to," I said, without even asking what they wanted me to do.

Ed told me they wanted me to do a series of 3-4 short comedy acts to break up the flow of the show. I would need to audition by showing them some of my material and then we would work out the details. My dad would be the emcee and I would be his sidekick.

At the time, Steve Martin was my hero, and he is still my favorite stand-up comic of all time. He is silly, smart and comes up with the craziest humor I've ever seen. I bet he would like my invisible wrestler. I had developed an entire repertoire of Steve Martin material complete with my own white suit, an "arrow through the head" prop, balloon animals and juggling. In other words, I stole his material and added a few of my own gags. Sorry Mr. Martin (As if Steve Martin is reading my book).

The theme of the Frolics that year was *Magic Moments*. Using the Steve Martin lines and some goofy magic tricks, I wowed the crowd with different comic bits. For instance, I did a card trick with miniature cards so no one in the audience could tell if I did it correctly. I pulled a rabbit out of a visor (the rabbit was very obviously fake and was pulled from a box under the visor) and I juggled. The finale came when I was supposed to tie my dad up and he would miraculously appear untied. But, I couldn't remember how to do the trick so he was wheeled off the stage while I closed the show. The crowd loved it.

In that instant, I was famous. The lights, the laughter and the applause were phenomenal. I had made an impression and people would surely remember me.

For the next few weeks, I was a celebrity all over town. People were congratulating me for my performance and telling me I was going to make it big. One woman, however, had watched me do the "fake" magic tricks and missed the point. She came up to my mother after the performance and said, "You tell Ronnie that if he keeps practicing, he'll be a good magician one day." She wouldn't remember me, but since she thought I had flopped big time, that's a good thing.

*   *   *   *   *

We all have a need to be remembered. We all have a yearning to make a difference. Can you think of a time you made people laugh? Remember how good that felt? Chances are, those people remember it too, and they remember it fondly. Sharing good humor is a way to become memorable. If you have a hankering to lead a life that matters, figure out how you can help the people around you have a good time.

The Emperor's Neck-ed

If you are going to tell people the truth,
you'd better make them laugh.
Otherwise they'll kill you.

– GB Shaw, playwright

I hate to be wrong. My therapist would say it's wrong to think like that. I hate that.

"There's nothing wrong with being wrong," he would say. I'm not totally sure but I think he may be wrong about that.

I admire people who can be wrong. They seem stronger. Wrong people can look at you and say, "You may be right." And they mean it. When I say, "You may be right," I really mean, "There's no way you're right but I can't quite figure out how you're wrong so I'll just pretend to be confident and gracious." I'm afraid being wrong means that people think I'm stupid or not worthy. I'm not sure where I got that idea but it is so deeply ingrained in my mind, I'm never wrong.

Last year, I took the Myers-Briggs Personality Inventory and found out something very revealing. All my life I have made reasonable decisions based on the facts and data before me. I have a very logical brain so I always liked to prove my decisions are based on sound evidence. But the Myers-Briggs showed me I don't use facts at all. Instead, I rely on intuition to make most decisions. What's worse, I often get facts wrong. Imagine that. All this time, I thought I was crafting courtroom style arguments with clear consistent information, when instead I was actually defending my position with data that had no basis in reality. Yikes. I was a fraud and never knew it.

Since I now know my decision making comes from intuition, I try to let go of the need to always be right. Instead, I live for the day when I can honestly say, "You may be right."

That's Sick

In my work as a hospice social worker, my primary role was to complete a psychosocial assessment of the patients and families to determine how they were coping and then provide counseling services to help them deal with their circumstances. When I used to tell people I worked in hospice care, they would inevitably say, "You must be special to do that kind of work." Whereas I am flattered anyone would consider me a special person, hospice work was not the depressing death-haunted experience many think it is. Instead, it was uplifting, rewarding and inspiring. I got to enter a person's life at a time they usually didn't want to welcome anyone new, and help them maneuver through their remaining days. I witnessed family members resolving life-long conflicts so there would be peace when a loved one died. Hospice was a profound experience, and yet there were times when it was also very funny.

As a home care social worker, I offered individual, family and group counseling in our patients' homes all over northern Virginia. One day, I was scheduled to visit a terminally ill man in Vienna. Upon his admission to our program, the hospice nurse had created a sheet of important patient information that included name, age, diagnosis, family contacts and driving directions to the patient's home. These directions were always accurate, because after the nurse wrote them down, the team secretary verified the directions by comparing them to a map. They were never wrong.

Except this time.

As I approached the street on which the patient lived, the directions said to take the "second left" off Maple Street. I should have taken the third left. Following the directions, I took the second left and began looking for the patient's house. To confirm I was on the right street, I always checked the house numbers as a point of reference. There was a major flaw in my reasoning though, because in this particular neighborhood, the house numbers were the same on every street! So, unbeknownst to me, I was on my way to visit a terminally ill patient and was approaching the wrong house!

I knocked on the door of the wrong house and was greeted by a kind-looking woman who was the approximate age of the patient's wife. I smiled and said, "Hi, I'm Ron Culberson, the hospice social worker."

Without missing a beat, the woman took a step back and said, "You know, I've got a cold, but I'm not *that* sick!"

At first, I didn't understand. I wondered how she could be this insensitive to her husband's condition. Then I wondered if she had lost touch with reality. As a trained mental health professional, my therapeutic "vision" equipped me to recognize psychotic behavior instantly. I began to look for other symptoms that would allow me to classify her through the *DSM IV Manual of Mental Disorders*. I was having trouble seeing any behavioral trend that would lead me to believe she was incompetent. Then it occurred to me. Could she be making a joke?

I am a trained humor professional and have honed my ability to see humor where others don't. But, every once in a while, I miss it. It just sails right over my head. I don't like admitting that, so I usually pretend to get the joke, even when I don't. I remember studying one *Far Side* cartoon for two-and-a-half days because I didn't get it. Rather than being duped, I was determined to stay with it until I got it. I finally did but never told anyone how long it took.

Not knowing whether I should begin a mental health assessment or barge in to make sure the patient was all right, I decided to take the passive approach and pretend nothing happened. So, I said, "I'm here to see Mr. Johnson (name changed to protect my guilt)."

"There is no one here by that name. That's why I responded to your first comment the way I did." She said, "I knew *I* didn't need a hospice social worker."

The physiological process of blushing begins when our brain tells us we just stepped in cow dung while wearing our brand new Reebok sandals. This leads to an immediate increase in blood flow to the capillaries in the face. Heat sensors quickly inform us we're embarrassed and our body recognizes it. I wonder what function this action serves. What would Darwin say is the survival function of blushing? Perhaps it's some sort of early warning system letting foes know our head is about to explode. Whatever the purpose, I'm sure I was fire-engine red that day.

The pressure in my head was increasing by the second but I avoided sure disaster by offering my own witty retort, "Good one."

I smiled, thanked my mystery humorist for understanding and backed all the way to my car. How did I make this mistake? Surely I didn't go to the wrong house. It couldn't have been my fault.

I called the office and told them what happened. I told them what the woman had said and I explained that either she or the nurse must have gotten the directions wrong. After about ten minutes of continuous laughter, the secretary said, "You may be right."

I Don't Get It

I rely on humor to help me in many social situations. John Purifoy and Dave Williams were two of my high school friends that got it. We saw humor in everything. We were always telling each other the newest joke we'd heard or pointing out something funny happening around us. To this day, we will see something funny and share a special connection that happens when we share an inside joke.

I was sort of a nerd in high school. Not the pen protector, techno-geek kind of nerd but a teacher's pet nerd. I made good grades, never got in trouble, and was in the band. I was probably every parent's dream but *not* the envy of my peers.

And forget about the girls.

When it came to dating, I was just unprofessional. I was polite and a gentleman but I really didn't know what I was doing. My hormones were raging and I dreamed of making out with the popular girls but they were only interested in the bad-boy athletes, not the good-boy baritone horn players. In time however, I did date some very nice girls. The problem was, they had a tough time relating to my natural wit. To be blunt, they didn't get it.

Let's say I was on a date with a lovely girl and we were riding somewhere in my parent's Chevy Malibu. I would engage in small talk and then say, "Want to hear a joke?"

"Sure," was always the response.

"This three-legged dog walked into an old west saloon and said, 'I'm looking for the man who shot my paw.'"

With a huge grin on my face, I would look over at my date and see a face with less expression than Al Gore.

"What's wrong?" I'd say.

"I didn't get it."

As I steered the car back onto the road, I would search for some sense that she was pulling my leg. But as I studied her face and the pinpoints of her pupils, I realized she was yet another humor dyslexic. The carefully crafted words that resulted in the excellent pun only sounded like a jumbled mish-mash of words to her. It was as if I had spoken Greek. The truth devastated me. I was dating one of them. An Unfunnite.

Being the gentleman I was, and not wanting to make fun of the humor-disabled, I would politely say, "It wasn't that good anyway" and explain that the word "paw" sounded like the word "pa," and it referred to the dog's foot *and* to its father. I would go on to say it was a reference to the days when an outlaw would be looking to revenge the death of his father.

"Oh," she would say.

As I dug the hole deeper, I would explain that the humor lies in two meanings of the word and it makes you consider the two possibilities. I tried to refrain from a lengthy discussion of the history of puns, figuring the basic explanation of the joke was enough for this go round. (In my humble opinion, explaining a joke is like kissing your grandmother on the lips. It won't kill you, but it just ain't right.)

I know my date certainly had no intentions of insulting me, but it was during times like this I realized how someone could drive a car off the edge of a 1,500 foot cliff.

How could she not see the humor? How could she not see the tremendous juxtaposition? If nothing else, how could she not laugh at a dog walking into a saloon?

Simply put, that was my life in high school. I went out with a few girls and I continuously explained jokes, realizing I was breaking the highest moral code of humorists.

In 1979, when I met Wendy, we were living in the same dorm at the University of Virginia. As I mentioned before, Wendy was beautiful, smart, and fun.

As I got to know her, I realized Wendy was probably too good for me. In high school, this type of girl would talk to me only if no one was looking. But Wendy was different. She seemed remotely interested in me even though our backgrounds could not have been more different. She grew up in Southampton, New York and I was raised in Emory, Virginia. She had been around the world. I had been around the Patricks' farm. She was cultured. I was simple. But as we got to know each other, my charm prevailed.

We started dating in February of 1980 after the infamous Valentine's dance. On one of our first dates, we were driving down the road and I said, "I've got a joke for you."

"Great," she said.

I got excited just thinking about her laughing.

"What did the fish say when it hit the concrete wall?"

"I don't know."

"Dam!"

I looked at her face expecting to see hysterics, passion, or at the very least, admiration, a just reward for my sharp wit. Instead, I saw something hauntingly familiar. I saw the pinpoint pupils. I saw a glazed-over expression. I saw disappointment.

Oh no. I thought. *She didn't get it.*

"You didn't get it?" I asked.

"No, I got it. I just didn't think it was funny."

At that moment, I was transported to the mountaintop. Blinded by the brilliant shine of enlightenment, I found myself unable to speak. This is it. I have found her. She must be the perfect woman and she is with me. I rejoiced. In the name of Charlie Chaplin, I silently professed my love for her, and on that evening knew Wendy Colclough would one day be my wife.

I proudly smiled and said, "You may be right."

* * * * *

Being wrong is not a death sentence. Being unable to admit it is. Can you think of a time you blew it big time? Did you have the courage to 'fess up? One of the best ways to face being wrong is by laughing at yourself. It helps you see the situation in a better light and puts the other people involved in a better mood. Self-deprecating humor can be the sugar that helps us swallow the medicine that makes us grow...up.

The Marriage of
Hugh Moore and Dee Stress

You can be late and upset,
or you can simply be late.
– Charlotte Davis Kasl, PhD, psychologist

The challenging thing about perspective is we often don't get it until after the fact. For instance, have you ever experienced a rude waiter or salesperson and you were left speechless? We always think of the perfect comeback—thirty minutes later. The healthy perspective always comes later, especially when you think you just made the biggest mistake of your life.

The setting was Great River, New York, a small town in central Long Island. The day was June 20, 1986. It was the day before I was to be married to the beautiful Wendy Colclough. I was a bit nervous. I was not nervous about getting married, I was nervous about the whole wedding gathering. You see, Wendy was from Long Island, about an hour east of New York City, and my family was from Emory, Virginia, a town of 280 people about an hour from nowhere. Our families were just a tad different and I was feeling some anxiety about their first meeting.

The nervousness got really bad the night before the wedding. The rehearsal was supposed to start at five o'clock and my family was to arrive around four. But, it was five and my family was not there. It got to be 5:15, 5:30 and then 5:45 and still no family. I had heard of the groom not showing up at the wedding, but not the groom's family.

We were trying to figure out why they weren't there and it occurred to us what must have happened. My family had planned to drive to Long Island that day from Southwest Virginia and had not timed their trip appropriately. In fact, they hit New York City just about 4:00 — on a Friday afternoon! During summer, that's the exact time everyone in New York City drives out to Long Island for the weekend. And Long Island was right where they were trying to "git."

The worst part of this was that my family was not familiar with traffic. They lived in a wide spot in the road, for heaven's sakes. The only traffic jam they had ever seen was when four people arrived at a four-way stop at the same time. They'd all be stuck there for twenty minutes because everyone was yelling, "No, you go ahead," "Oh no, please, you go ahead."

Realizing my parents might be caught in the unbelievable New York traffic, I envisioned them taking a wrong turn into New York City. I just had this image in my head of…well…of Jed, Granny and Ellie Mae going right down to the middle of Manhattan. And I knew what would happen next. My father, then the Vice President of Emory & Henry College, was a "meet and greet" kind of guy. He was a former college recruiter and was always doing that PR thing. I knew he would pull up to the curb somewhere in Manhattan. He would get out, put on his sports jacket and walk up to the first person he saw. He would extend his hand and say, "Connie Culberson, from Emory and Henry College. Do you know where the Colclough wedding is?"

I started to sweat but they finally arrived.

My family finally got there about 6:00, but we missed most of the rehearsal. Our pastor said, "Just do your best."

The rest of the evening was uneventful. The rehearsal dinner went well and a number of people stood up and gave little speeches. In fact, my father talked about how lucky I was to marry Wendy. Since she had made all A's at the University of Virginia, my father made some wise-crack about my finally bringing home A's! After a great evening with family and friends, we retired to the Ramada Inn in Hauppauge about 11:30 p.m.

The hotel was 30 minutes from the church. That night, I had two options for my accommodations. I could sleep on a cot in my parents' room or I could sleep in the same room with my good friend Dave Linkous. Even though my parents thought I should have stayed with them (a little last minute bonding before the wedding, I guess), I chose to stay with Dave.

We got into our beds by midnight and cut off the light. At that instant, we realized we had forgotten to close the curtain because we could see the light from the Amoco station next door. So, I got up and closed the curtain. The minute I did, the room went pitch black. The curtain had thick rubber insulation on the back and it blocked out every bit of light. I couldn't even see to get back to my bed.

I asked Dave to turn the light back on and said, "Wow, that's dark. Wouldn't it be funny if it was so dark in the morning, I didn't wake up in time?"

I knew there was no way I would sleep late because the wedding was at 11:00 a.m. so I went to bed without a second thought….and slept very soundly.

The next morning, I was awakened by a noise in the room. The room was dark, I couldn't see a thing. I turned on the light and saw Dave walking around the room looking for something.

"What are you doing?" I asked.

"I'm looking for a clock. We didn't get our wakeup call."

"That's OK, my watch is right here on the bedside table."

I picked up my watch and looked at it. Twenty to eleven!

(May I remind you the wedding was at 11:00 and we were 30 minutes from the church?!)

I came out of bed so fast, my underwear stayed in the bed. It was a good thing, too, because it wasn't usable any more!

Without even thinking, I put on a clean pair (tighty whities in case you're visualizing) and headed out into the hallway to find someone to go to the church and tell them I was on my way. I ran down the hall hitting doors and screaming, "Somebody help me! Help me please!"

About halfway down the hall, it occurred to me. *Everybody's gone. They would have left 20 minutes ago to be there on time.* This put me in a panic. I started yelling and cursing and ran back into the room.

I slid into the bathroom and turned on the shower.

I thought, *I don't have time to take a shower.*

I turned off the shower.

Then a voice in my head said, *Man, you're getting married. You have to take a shower!*

I turned on the shower.

I found myself in what I call a "stress cycle" that was spiraling out of control. I started running back and forth saying, "Shower. No. Shower. No." All along, Dave was watching this, thinking he's witnessing his first psychiatric commitment.

Finally, I think he got a bit worried. This big vein on my head was getting bigger and my eyes had a rabid look to them. I think Dave was afraid I might have a heart attack. He grabbed me by the shoulders and with all his strength said, "Ron, calm down. Settle down......It's only 7:30, I set your watch ahead."

They never found Dave's body (just kidding).

* * * * *

Can you think of a time things started going south and you over-reacted? Did it help? Isn't it true that when we look back on things that panicked us, they often seem funny in hind-sight? Why wait? Why not find the funny now?

Kum Bah Humbug

Everything is within walking
distance if you have the time.
– Steven Wright, comedian

When in physical pain, we may receive a prescription for a medicine like Percocet to give us a false "perspective" that everything is just fine. It somehow numbs the portion of our brain that says, YOU'RE GOING TO DIE, YOU'LL NEVER SURVIVE THIS! When in emotional pain, humor can become the medicine that gives us the funny perspective to survive what we're going through.

I experienced real pain very early in my life (long before the kidney stone). My pain came in the form of a bone poking through my leg. On October 10, 1971, I was ten years old. That morning I had skipped church, a decision I would later regret, and had chosen to join my friends at the local pool hall for a few games of Eight Ball. We lived in the community surrounding Emory and Henry College and the local pool hall was actually the recreation center at the college. My dad was an administrator and my friends were professors' kids so we got to use the college facilities for free. However, it *was* a Methodist college and we should have been in church.

After a few hours of pool, I was walking the one-half mile from the college to my house. It was a gray fall day and looked as if it could rain at any moment. I was cold and wanted a ride home. Even though the walk was not that long, I was basically lazy and jumped at the chance to expend less energy whenever possible.

As I got within a few hundred yards of my house, I heard a car coming behind me. I turned to see who it was. In a small town like ours, you almost always knew who was driving on your patch of road. If it was someone I knew, I'd get a ride home in the warm comfort of their car.

Not recognizing the driver, I turned back toward my destination. In an instant, I saw a flash of blue and then the lights went out. A few seconds later, I came to in the ditch. I had no idea what happened and my brain was foggier than the weather. I raised my head and I looked down at my right leg. It was bent at a right angle and wedged under my left leg. The shoe on my left leg was gone. As I continued trying to figure out what had happened, I noticed a hole in my right pants leg in the center of my thigh and there was pink "stuff" coming out of it. Then I realized I couldn't move my leg.

I had been hit by a car which had broken the femur bone in my thigh. The car knocked me into the air, where I somersaulted and landed in the ditch. Apparently, the car broke my leg and the force of the landing then pushed the bone back through my skin and pants. This was not good. Most adults would have been a bit concerned at this point. As a ten-year old, I lost it! Although I was in shock and not in a great deal of pain at the moment, I was sure I was going to die.

Using the fullest available lung power, I began to scream. I screamed at the people who stopped to help me. I screamed at my dad and brother who ran down from the house to help me. I screamed at everybody.

When the volunteer paramedics arrived, they quickly realized they needed to cut my pants to relieve the swelling in my leg. When the dude came at me with a pair of scissors, I was sure he was going to cut my leg off. In hindsight, I understand that not only would it have been a major challenge trying to cut my leg off with a pair of scissors, he wouldn't have done it in front of all the bystanders. But in times like that, rationality goes out the window. So, in my fractured state of mind, I screamed at him. Finally, he was so frightened by my psychotic behavior, he backed off.

As the paramedics were getting me on the stretcher and into the back of the ambulance, my minister happened to drive by.

Great, I thought, *he's going to remind me that this is what happens if you don't go to church.*

He only spoke to my father for a moment and then headed up to my house. My mother was alone and my dad felt my minister could be a support to her. Bad idea. Picture this. Your youngest child, who's only ten years old, just got hit by a car. They won't let you go see him and they tell you to stay in the house. For 20 minutes, you're pacing around not knowing what's happening. Then the minister walks in.

I heard my mother scream from inside the ambulance. Birds flew out of the trees and a wine glass on our neighbors' shelves shattered. I guess it serves my minister right for even thinking I should have been in church. Oh wait; I was the one who thought that. Never mind.

As soon as the ambulance got me to the hospital, people started rushing around trying to organize my care. The worst part of the experience came when they x-rayed my leg. In order to see things properly, they had to straighten my still bent and broken right leg. Being in shock no longer protected me from the pain. It was so excruciating, I thought I was going to faint. So I screamed at the x-ray technician.

They gave me pain medicine, which started to work after a few minutes. In addition to my broken leg and the hole in my thigh, I had a bruised bone in my arm and a cut on my hip. Not too bad for getting hit by a car. They cut my clothes off and began cleaning up all the wounds. They washed my hip and used a big turkey baster to clean inside the hole in my leg. Then they stitched up my leg.

The doctor explained that when the bone broke, it shifted up towards my hip. In order for it to heal properly, they would have to pull it back down. They used "traction" to do this.

Traction involves gradually pulling on the bone until it is in the correct position to heal. In my case, they had to drill a pin through the bone below my knee. The pin would be attached to ropes strung over a pulley placed above my bed leading down to weights, which hung at the foot of the bed. A large gauze-covered ring was placed around my leg near my hip and then attached to the head of my bed. In essence, I had been put in the racks and my right leg was being stretched out. Am I grossing you out yet?

Needless to say, my first few nights in the hospital were miserable. I was vomiting, I couldn't get comfortable, and I kept having muscle spasms in my leg. Muscle spasms occur when a muscle relaxes and then tightens up. I would just about be asleep when my leg would jump off the bed. Of course, I screamed for the nurse when this happened.

I was supposed to be in traction for five weeks. I thought there was no way I was going to make it.

During my stay, I had several roommates. My second room-mate happened to be the son of the president of the local volunteer rescue squad. One day, my roommate's dad came over to my bed. The paramedic who had tried to cut my pants was there to visit my roommate. He was afraid to come in the room because I might freak out. Now that's funny. It turns out he was a very nice guy and my screaming had really traumatized him. We eventually became friends.

Pediatric units of hospitals are popular places for community groups. They want to cheer up the poor children in the hospital, so they often visit, bringing toys and in general, doing everything they can to make your stay a little bit brighter. One particular Sunday evening about seven o'clock, 15 girls from the Calvary Baptist Church youth choir visited all of us sick kids in the hospital. This gaggle of girls crowded around my hospital bed and announced they were here to cheer me up. I'm ten. A room full of girls is not likely to cheer me up. But, being a polite kid, I smiled and thanked them for coming.

The choir director blew into her "pitch finder" and the girls began to sing *Kum Bah Yah*. At first I thought, this isn't so bad. They're pretty good. A couple of them were even kind of cute. They finished the first verse and launched into verse two. After that, I had just started to clap when I realized they were starting another verse. Verse three rolled right into four which segued into five, six and seven. By eight o'clock, I had endured 27 verses of *Kum Bah Yah*. I will remind you I was tied to the bed with no escape. Finally, the girls left and I pried my lips loose from the paralyzed smile on my face. I called the nurse and asked for a pain pill. To this day, I need an aspirin to get through even one verse of Kum Bah Yah.

People were fascinated with my traction. My leg was in this giant sling and I had ropes attached to me in several different places. Every week they would add additional weights to the system so it would continue to pull the bone in my leg into the proper position.

During week three, my sister-in-law Ede came to visit. She asked, "What's this?"

I said, "What's what?"

Then, she lifted the weights on the end of the bed and said, "These weights."

I think my response was, "HOLY CRAP, PUT THOSE DOWN, THEY'RE ATTACHED TO THE BONE IN MY LEG!!!"

I can't blame her for being frightened, I was frightened too. But…she…didn't have…to…drop…the…weights.

"ΛΛΛΛΛΛΛΛΛΛΛΛΛΛΛΛΛHHHHHHHHHHHHHH!" I screamed.

Ede has never forgiven me for that, and I've never let her forget it.

Finally I got to come home from the hospital. But the ordeal wasn't over. The bone was now in the proper place and it had to heal. So they put a huge cast on my leg. It went from the ankle on my right foot to my belly button and back down to the knee on my left leg. It had a big hole in the middle so I could use a bedpan.

I was so glad to be home. My dad carried me into the dining room (my new bedroom) and put me into the rented hospital bed. I leaned back on the pillow and noticed the sign on the wall: *WELOME HOME RONNIE!*

"Welome?" I said, "What does welome mean?"

This time, everybody screamed…with laughter (for a change).

*   *   *   *   *

Bruce Springsteen once said "Someday we'll look back on this and it will all seem funny." When traumatic events occur, we have a choice to lighten the situation with humor. Laughter makes every situation better and looking back on those situations with humor makes the memories sweeter. Think back to something you've experienced that was traumatic at the time. Any way you could get some *smileage* out of it by realizing it may have been screamingly funny?

Cutting Up

Disappointment is cured by
revamped expectations.

– Max Lucado, author

Sometimes the perspective we need is right behind us. But we're so focused on what's ahead of us, we don't see the big picture. I guess that means *blind*sight is not 20:20.

When I turned 30, I realized for the first time that I was losing my hair. I had never really checked the back of my head. Then, one fateful day, I looked in the mirror and noticed this big bald spot, and it was growing.

I said to my wife, "Why didn't you tell me?"

"We thought you knew," she responded.

From that point on, I hated getting my hair cut. First of all, I was paying about $14 plus a tip every month but these people, professional hair stylists, were doing less and less work. That wasn't right. On top of that, so to speak, I was just downright embarrassed to have someone working on my bald spot. It's a personal place that should only be touched by the owner and a medical professional.

I was whining about this to a friend one day and he said, "Why don't you cut your own hair?"

I had never considered this. *Hmmm. Cut my own hair?* I actually liked the concept. I would be in control. I would touch my bald spot the way I wanted to and I would not be paying these "perm pirates" more then they deserved.

My friend told me to go to Wal-Mart and I would find a nice selection of electric clippers for about $25. This was great. Since I was paying $14 plus tip every month, I could mangle my head for two months and the clippers would be paid for. The next day, I went to Wal-Mart and found the shelf where the clippers were. They had all kinds, different models, different sizes and different accessories. They were all about $25.

Except one.

The Conair 5.3 horsepower clippers. Wow. This bad boy was loaded. It had two combs, a pair of scissors, hair clips, an instructional video, a quart of oil, a nice plastic gown to put over my shoulders so the hair doesn't get on me, a little brush to sweep off my neck and about a dozen different blade guards for different depths and styles. Now here's the kicker. This "hair cutlery system" was usually $30 but was on sale for $25. I closed the deal.

I went home, put in the video and watched as the narrator explained how "easy it is to cut your hair." He said, "Simply choose the blade guard you want based on the style and thickness of your desired cut and then attach it to the clippers. Turn the clippers on and while running the clippers against your head in an upward fashion, rock your wrist backward in smooth rolling manner. *Just like flipping pancakes*, I thought. By following these instructions, your hair will be cut evenly and stylishly."

I'm thinking to myself, *I've got a Master's degree and have certainly flipped pancakes. Piece of cake.*

So I plugged my Conair 5.3 horsepower clippers in, attached the #4 blade guard and began to rock my wrists while running the clippers up my head. I went all over my head and to my amazement; the clippers cut my hair evenly all over. It was too simple. It looked like I had paid a professional to cut my hair.

I quickly realized I had two problems with this new process. I couldn't really see the back of my neck well and it was hard for me to trim around my ears. I knew I couldn't do a decent job, considering it was so hard to reach both of these locations. So I asked my wife for help. She was glad to assist and by the time she was done, it looked like I had paid at least $16 for my haircut.

For the next five months, I cut my own hair and was darn pleased with the money I was saving. During the sixth month, I had a speaking engagement in Minneapolis for the Ronald McDonald Charities' regional conference. I was the opening keynote speaker for 400 conference attendees. The conference coordinator told me that since I was the opening speaker, I would be setting the tone for their entire conference. It was quite an honor and I took the responsibility very seriously.

The night before my trip, I was packing my suitcase. While organizing my toiletry bag, I looked in the mirror and realized I needed a haircut. As I had done for the five months before, I got my Conair clippers out, attached the #4 blade guard and using that rocking motion of my wrist, I cut my hair. Then I asked my wife to help me out. Just like I had done before, I took the blade guard off, handed her the clippers and asked her to "clean up my neck."

Somehow, on that particular night, she misunderstood. My wife, the woman I love, the mother of my two children and my soul partner took those razor sharp electric clippers without the

#4 blade guard attached, stuck them in the center of my head and took one swipe down.

All I heard was a very somber, "Oh no."

If you have never had someone rake electric clippers to the back of your head and then exclaim, "Oh no," let me assure you it will send a chill up your spine like you have never experienced. I spun around and said, "What do you mean, 'Oh no'?"

At this point she was running.

"Oh, no. Oh, no. Oh, no," she was saying.

Now, I panicked. I grabbed the little handheld mirror and looked at the back of my head in the big mirror.

Oh no.

From the base of my bald spot to the skin on my neck was a bare vertical strip of skin with not one bit of hair in it. It was a reverse Mohawk. It looked like my bald spot had an exit ramp!

Now, we're both panicked. We're running around the room saying, "What are we going to do? What are we going to do?"

I said. "I've got a keynote address tomorrow and I've got a hole in the back of my head!"

When the adrenaline in our systems had reached a saturation point, we stumbled into that state of shock where the brain, in its attempt to be helpful, gets creative even though it is not functioning on all four cylinders. We got a great idea.

We'll cut up, we thought.

In other words, we decided to cut the portion of my hair from the base of my neck up towards the top of my head so the bare vertical strip was shorter and less obvious. It seemed like a marvelous plan at the time.

After Wendy used her best pruning skills to raise the base of my hairline, it became ridiculously obvious we had failed to take into consideration one important detail. I am pale to begin with. I am very pale. I'm so pale; I am almost devoid of color. I have to use number 30 sun block when I'm in a room with more than one fluorescent light.

When we cut up, so to speak, we had exposed even more of my scalp to the light. I now had a vertical *and* horizontal strip of pale skin! It looked like I had received some sort of neuro-logical research grant.

Then I thought, *the folks at the Ronald McDonald Chari-ties work with cancer patients. They're going to think that I've had chemotherapy or something. This is just not right.*

It was awful. My guilt-ridden wife spent a couple of hours trying to make it better. A snip here, a snip there. No luck. It still looked awful. Finally, at about 11:00 that night, I said, "That's it. I can't take this anymore. I have to stop working on this and get to bed. I'm too stressed out."

Then it occurred to me. *Wait a minute. I'm the man. I'm the humor guy. I'm the one going all over the country telling people to lighten up and to not let stress get them down. If anyone can deal with this situation, it has to be me.*

It was at that point that I made an important discovery about humor and adversity. A discovery that changed the way I think and live. I discovered that in times of tremendous stress, this humor theory is full of crap!

There was nothing I could do to get this stress out of my mind.

I couldn't sleep a bit that night because my pillow felt like a block of ice. The back of my head was now very sensitive.

On the plane to Minneapolis the next morning, I was trying to relax and distract myself when I looked around and thought, *Is every air vent turned toward me? It's like a wind tunnel in here!*

Then the flight attendant came by.

"Would you like a beverage sir?"

"Why yes, I'll have a Coke."

She turned to get my Coke and when she was handing it to me, the cup slipped a bit in her hand.

"Wow that was a close shave," she said.

In my best Charlie Brown voice, I said, "Ugggggghhhh!"

It was like this all the way up to the start of my presentation. All these reminders were making me painfully aware of the Grand Canyon on the back of my head. Five minutes before my presentation, I was a mess. I couldn't concentrate and realized I had to do something in order to focus. Just before I was introduced, I made the decision to start my presentation with the story of my haircut. I figured by getting it out there, it would relieve me of the stress of covering it up.

It worked. But I embellished the end of the story. I said, "Now, I have a new perspective. When I get back to my office, I'm going to change all of my marketing materials so everything I send out says, "Ron Culberson, A *Cut* Above The Rest!" The audience roared and for the first time, I felt the stress leave my body. And the best part of the whole experience came after my presentation when 15 people came up front to see my head up close!

Unbeknownst to me, the humor was right behind me all along.

*   *   *   *   *

Can you think of a time you were anxious or fearful, and you decided to "tell the truth" and it bonded you with others? Humor has the power to bring us together, if we let it. It builds bridges instead of walls. If you're feeling ashamed or self-conscious about something and you're keeping it to yourself, you're robbing yourself of the opportunity to connect with others and share a laugh about the absurdity of the human condition.

Help Yourself to Some Humor

I, not events, have the power to make me happy or unhappy today. I can choose which it shall be. Yesterday is dead, tomorrow hasn't arrived yet. I have just one day, today, and I'm going to be happy in it.

– Groucho Marx, comedian

Viktor Frankl suffered the atrocities of three concentration camps in World War II. As described in his classic book, *Man's Search for Meaning*, Frankl discovered "the last of the human freedoms is to choose one's attitude in any given set of circumstances." Having survived that horrific experience, he chose not to become a bitter man. He spent the rest of his life sharing his philosophy that while we may not be able to control events, we can control how we respond to those events.

Sometimes, the way we choose to respond is not the most productive response, and it leads us into a much greater predicament. For example, my dad was not one to do anything which he felt would impose on others.

I was home for the summer between my second and third year of college, and I woke up at 2:00 a.m. to a low moan coming from my parents' bathroom. My parents are much older than me. They are now in their 80s and everything seems to be falling apart—shoulders, knees, eyes. While, they say the first thing to go is your memory, it's not. The first thing to go is your bowels—it's just that when your memory goes, you forget your bowels went first.

So, back in 1981, when things started to go for my parents, a moan coming from the bathroom was not uncommon. I just assumed it was their "usual" bathroom routine, especially since we had eaten chili, broccoli and coleslaw for dinner. Now that I'm an adult, I realize that this combination was the colonic equivalent of Mt. Saint Helens. So, I went back to sleep assuming one of my parents couldn't sleep and was just passing "time" and not much else in the bathroom.

I woke up again at 4:00 a.m. to an even louder moan. Now, my mind started playing tricks on me. I got up to see what was going on in the bathroom. This little voice in my head that had seen too many scary movies warned me to be cautious as I approached the bathroom, in case I found a wild dog or an escapee from the mental asylum holed up in there. I know it sounds crazy, but I read a lot of Stephen King.

The closer I got to the bathroom, the more the wild dog sounded like my dad. I knocked on the door and said, "Are you alright?"

He didn't respond so I said it again. He still didn't respond so I pushed the door open to find my dad lying on the floor.

My father comes from the generation of men who never ask for help because they don't want to "impose." He would routinely try to lift things that were too heavy for three grown men while grunting, "I've got it" or he would eat an entire meal he didn't order to avoid imposing on the waitress. I'm sure that's why he had stayed in the bathroom for so long. He did not want to bother my mom or me.

Clearly he was in a tremendous amount of pain so I asked, "What's wrong?"

In between moans, he said, "Nothing…I'll…be…alright?"

Right.

Here is where my dad and I are different. I always ask for help and don't mind imposing on anybody if I need to get something done. I'll ask for directions, I'll ask for help picking out clothes to wear, and I'll even ask for help with my deep-seeded emotional issues. Therapists *love* me. I immediately woke my mom, who had apparently been sleeping on her "good ear" (long story) and explained what was going on.

She told me to call an ambulance. I picked up the phone and there was no dial tone. At this point, the Stephen King thing came back and I started to panic—someone had obviously slipped my father a Mickey and then cut the phone line. OK, so I have an active imagination. Remember, this was southwest Virginia and our imaginations gave us some of the only entertainment available.

Turns out our phone had been out for a couple of days. So I ran next door and woke up our neighbors, the Binghams. You can already see the difference between my dad and me. I had been awake for only five minutes and I had imposed on four other people. Now that I think about it, I'm just plain annoying.

I called the rescue squad (pre-911 days) and told the dispatcher we needed an ambulance, fast. She asked for directions to our house.

I said, "Take the interstate to exit 9 and turn left at Meadowview Elementary School. Then, turn right at Ryan's store and go about one mile. After DeVault's Trailer Park, we are the third house on the right."

She said, "Is that the Culberson's house?"

I said, "Yeah."

She said, "Who's this?"

"This is Ronnie Culberson."

She said, "Hey Ronnie, this is Mary Carter, what are you up to?"

"Not much," I said, "I'm just home from school and my dad's got this problem."

"Really," she said, "How's school?"

"Fine, but I think I need to get an ambulance for my dad right now."

Small towns.

I told Mary my dad had an intense pain in his side and had been on the floor of the bathroom for several hours.

She said, "Why didn't he call sooner?"

I told her I didn't have time to explain my dad's "impose-a-phobia." She said she would send an ambulance right away.

I hung up and then called Dr. Ashworth, our family doctor (imposition number six in case you're keeping track). He said it sounded like my dad might have a kidney stone, and he'd be right over. That's the beauty of a small town. People come right over.

Dr. Ashworth arrived shortly before the ambulance. He assessed the situation and was quite sure my dad had a kidney stone. We got my dad back to bed, and Dr. Ashworth gave him a shot of Demerol.

The ambulance arrived next accompanied by three four-wheel drive vehicles (impositions 7-10). The new participants were rescue squad volunteers who had heard the call come in on their scanners (it's scary to think they were listening to their scanners at 4:00 a.m.). When they heard the dispatcher describe the call as a "possible heart attack," they came to help.

One of these guys said, "We know your dad, and wanted to help if we could."

At this point, my dad had begun to loosen up in more ways than one. He thanked Dr. Ashworth and the guys multiple times and, of course, apologized for the imposition.

Once he was securely blanketed and strapped onto the stretcher, they rolled his loopy self into the back of ambulance. With all the commotion, a crowd had gathered in the front yard. The Hayters, the Patricks and some guy who was out for a walk (imposition 11-15) were all there. We reassured them everything was under control and prepared for the ride to the hospital. My mom took her rightful spot in the back of the ambulance and I drove my car behind it.

One mile down the road, the ambulance missed the turn to the interstate.

Surely they were not taking the "scenic" route to the hospital.

This route would add another 10 minutes to the trip and I was surprised they did not go the quicker way. After another mile down the road, the ambulance took a sharp left turn into the parking lot of the Shady Manor Rest Home. Shady Manor was one of roughly 300 nursing homes in my town. For some reason, we had one of the largest per capita concentrations of nursing homes in the country. That probably makes it the denture capital of the world. I'm very proud.

Now, I was starting to become concerned. Since when did they take someone with a kidney stone directly to long term care? I got out of the car and asked the driver what was going on. He said they had received a call about a nursing home patient in distress and since my dad was now comfortable, they decided to check it out. After about 15 minutes, the rescue squad dudes came out with someone on another stretcher and they put the person in the back with my dad! It was like an Amtrak ambulance…"All aboard!"

We finally got to the hospital. By that time, my dad was fully loaded with Demerol.

Did I mention he was on the hospital board of directors? You can imagine the treatment he got. The administrator of the hospital came down immediately to see if my dad was all right. My dad started talking business without having any idea what he was saying. He just kept saying, "I don't want to impose."

The administrator, who was quite a cutup, told everyone in the ER my dad was being treated for "VD." At this point, with only a few hours of sleep, I felt like I was in an episode of the *Twilight Zone*.

My poor dad suffered with his kidney stones for nine more days until he finally passed them. He never forgot the misery. The following year, he was in the hospital again for a recurrence of kidney stones. Turns out, in an attempt to be helpful, my mother had been giving him calcium supplements which grew another set of stones.

My dad refers to that as the "year she tried to kill me."

Now that's an imposition.

* * * * *

Are your usual responses to life making you a pain in the…side? Give yourself and others a break by not getting too caught up in the significance of you. By allowing yourself to be vulnerable, you allow others to serve. When we choose to see our frailties, we really do know freedom and then can have some fun with our shortcomings. Help yourself to some humor and *lighten* the load of those around you

Dentally III

*For there was never yet a philosopher
that could endure the toothache patiently.*

– William Shakespeare, playwright

The dentist's office is the epitome of stress. No matter what my dentist or his assistant is doing in my mouth, it's uncomfortable. My legs and arms are always tired when I leave his office, because I am tense for so long. My chiropractor could actually go into a partnership with my dentist. But imagine what it must be like to work in a dentist's office, where every patient you see doesn't want to be there. That's stress. Humor would go a long way in a dental practice.

My dentist is not known for his sense of humor. He doesn't even use laughing gas. Sorry. So when I went in for my first extraction (that's dentist talk for ripping a tooth and its roots from your jaw), I was not expecting stand-up comedy. I've had a lot of cavities in my life but never an extraction. Even the word made me nervous. "Extraction" implies some sort of organized technical excursion deep into the recesses of my mouth where teams of highly trained professionals would dig out the bad tooth as an example to the rest of the teeth to straighten up or else. Being on the receiving end of that excursion did not excite me. I have no need to discipline my other teeth by using one as an example. Yet there I was in the seat, being prepared for this first-ever experience.

Being the talkative motivational speaker that I am, I always engage in chatty pre-surgical dialogue with anyone that will listen.

"So," I said, "what are you actually going to do?"

"Well," said my dentist, "I'll give you some Novocain. Not too much though because this is not a difficult procedure. Then, when it takes effect, I'll use a special type of pliers to pull out the tooth. It should be easy. I'm really good at this." He smiled.

The warning bells were already ringing in my head. "Feel free to use as much Novocain as you need," I replied.

"Don't worry. It will be fine."

He gave me a shot of Novocain and left the room while it took effect. He came back a few minutes later to see if it was working.

"I can still feel my jaw," I told him.

"I think it's good enough to start."

I was thinking, *I should be the judge of that! Sure, he's had dental school and years of practice, but I think I know the nerves in my mouth better than he does. I don't see the need for any unnecessary suffering. I don't pay him good money to make me hurt.* Of course, I didn't say any of these things out loud. My mind just thought them at a very rapid rate.

He leaned the chair back so the loose saliva in my mouth could work its way down to my gag reflex and then loaded my mouth with those small cotton Tootsie Rolls. Once my mouth was completely packed, he said to his assistant, "Elevator and forceps."

"Now, Ron," he said, "I will check in with you several times to see if you're comfortable. Do not hesitate to let me know if you're feeling any pain."

"Oh-Ay," I garbled.

After about 30 seconds of twisting and pulling, he said, "This is a little tougher than I expected. Are you OK?"

"Huh-huh," I managed. I was fine but I was beginning to feel the slightest bit of pain. I did not want this to become worse, so I focused on it to make sure it didn't.

He twisted and pulled a bit more. That time I was sure I felt something. *That's enough. I'm going to let him know that it's starting to hurt a bit.*

"I have just a bit more work, Ron." He said, "How are you doing?"

"Wewl," I said, "U'm star-un oo feew a bit uh some-un."

With that, he said, "Hold out your hand."

I didn't understand this. Was this some new pain control process? Maybe it was a nerve block or acupuncture. Why would he need my *hand*? I held it out anyway.

He dropped the tooth into my hand and said, "I told you I was good at this."

Sometimes we don't appreciate humor until much later. The stress of the circumstances often blocks our humor gland from working. That must have happened that day at the dentist. I attempted a weak smile but just couldn't get a laugh out.

In hindsight, it was really funny.

I think if we were more accustomed to fun and humor in difficult situations like that, we would be more open to it. But if we're not expecting it, it catches us off guard and flies under our laughter radar.

I now realize my dentist did a great thing by misleading me. If I had known the procedure would have been so quick, then any problem would have sent me to anxiety heaven. I guess my dentist knew what he was doing.

* * * * *

Have you ever had to go through an extractive process with someone—a situation you knew would cause them a bit of pain? Imagine how they would feel if you used some humor as your Novocain. Try surprising others with *humorelief* when times get tough. You may get to the *root* of the problem a lot easier.

Their Cup Was Half Full

If work was more fun,
it would feel less like work.

– Herb Kelleher, former CEO Southwest Airlines

Enjoying humor starts with a positive attitude that says we can enjoy our adult lives as much as we did when we were children. But the workplace has plenty of room for improvement when it comes to having fun.

My friend Jef Kahn is a master at using humor as an adult. It seems he continually has an attitude of fun lurking behind every behavior. He lived in a commune during the seventies. One of the requirements of joining the commune was to leave "worldly" things behind and take on a new identity. This required that each new *communee* take a new name. He changed his name from Jeff to Jef. He's brilliant and my hero.

Jef and I worked at Blue Ridge Hospital, which was part of the University of Virginia's Medical Center and housed the psychiatric unit of the hospital. We were mental health workers which was the State of Virginia's title for glorified aides. We all had bachelor's degrees but no advanced training in mental health.

The staff on this unit was mostly young men and women who enjoyed their jobs and had a lot of fun with one another. Practical jokes were commonplace and many were quite elaborate. For instance, we would create a fake medical record showing that a seriously insane patient was on his/her way to the hospital just to create anxiety for whoever was up for the next admission. Or we would put KY Jelly on the earpiece of the phone and then tell someone they had a call. When they answered the phone, the jelly would get in their ear.

I can imagine what you're thinking. Yes, it *was* hard at times to tell the patients from the staff.

Once, Jef and another friend John Hoyle were involved in a heated argument about the power of meditation. John, who was a student of eastern philosophies, swore one could become so adept at meditation he could drink his own urine without any damage to his body. Jef tended to be more pragmatic and basically told John he was full of "it." The argument continued with each getting more and more agitated.

I must admit I enjoyed watching my two friends go at it. Both Jef and John were pretty laid back and this was unlike anything I had ever seen them do. At one point during the argument, Jef pulled a 50 dollar bill out of his wallet and said, "OK, if you think this actually works, I'll give you 50 bucks to drink this urine." He pulled a sample of a patient's urine from the shelf and gave it to John. John looked queasy and said he was not completely confident in his own meditation skills. So as a compromise, he said he wouldn't drink it but would hold it in his mouth for 30 seconds. Jef agreed but reduced the bet to $20.

A crowd of staff had now gathered.

John uncapped the jar and recoiled at the smell. He raised the cup slowly to his lips and took a mouthful.

I felt the lunch in my stomach start to work its way back to the place where we first met. I ran from the nurse's station, sure I was going to lose it. A few dry heaves later, I felt better. I returned to the nurse's station to find Jef and John settling their bet. Jef threw the twenty at John and stormed out of the room.

This had gone much too far. They were very angry with each other.

Being the peacemaker I was and calling on my mental health skills, I told John to meet me in the large conference room while I went to find Jef. I figured I would try to smooth things over between them. These were two of my best friends and I didn't want them to be at odds. When Jef and I joined John in the conference room, I told them I felt they had taken this argument way too far and they needed to resolve the hurt feelings between them.

All at once, both of them started laughing.

"You've been had, Ron," Jef said.

At first, it didn't register. I couldn't figure it out. Then John explained that the entire drama had been staged and all the other staff members had been in on it. The urine was apple juice and it had all been at my expense.

I smiled weakly, as I felt my stomach turn one more time.

A total of seven people were in on this joke. I have to admit it was great day in the history of humor. To this day, we still talk about the "urine the money" joke.

That hospital was a special place to work. Those people and their priceless sense of humor were a gift in my life.

*   *   *   *   *

Now, you may not like "bathroom humor." You may think that practical joke was tasteless (more apologies). The point is, we're still talking about that practical joke decades later. Humor, by its very nature, demands we occasionally stretch the boundaries. If we spend 40 to 60 hours a week involved in dull, boring work, we are in danger of becoming dull and boring. Injecting a little fun will make work less work.

Thou Shalt Not Committee

If we can laugh at it, we can live with it.

– Erma Bombeck, humorist

When we interact with other people on and off the job, it's easy to get consumed by the conflicts that result from the different personalities. But if we create an atmosphere of enjoyable cooperation at work, at home, and in our community activities, who knows what the possibilities can be.

Church committees may be the closest thing to hell on earth we'll ever experience. Don't get me wrong. I love my church and I love the people in my church. But church committees *can* bring out the worst in people. As explained before, I belong to the Presbyterian Church USA denomination. We're the more moderate of the Presbyterian churches—not really liberal, not too conservative. Yet, it is still a church, and in a church you have people who think their opinions are revelations from God. That perspective can create some very heated discussions.

Once, we had a Coffee Committee. That's right, a Coffee Committee. This group was charged with deciding whether to have our coffee catered or to have volunteers in the church come in at the crack of dawn on Sundays to make coffee for 800 people in our 400-year-old coffee urns. This committee was also given the challenge of determining *where* to serve coffee—in the vestibule where the brand new carpet had been installed, or in the fellowship hall which was just far enough away from the sanctuary that some people wouldn't walk to it. See where this is going?

For two years, the members of the Coffee Committee battled each other and the members of the congregation. I was convinced coffee beans must come from the Tree of Knowledge (you know, the forbidden tree in the Garden of Eden) or else it would have never created this much trouble. Eventually the issue was resolved and all is well with coffee in our church. Even so, I can still walk up to the former chair of this committee and say "decaf" and she'll break out in hives. Church committees can be a challenge to say the least.

In their infinite desire to follow God's will and help others, church members sometimes get so caught up in the procedures of the church they miss the mission of the church. I served a three-year term as a Deacon and saw this happen at every meeting.

The Deacons in our church were like social workers. We responded to financial requests from members of the congregation and to people in the community who might need a meal, a place to stay, or transportation. The Deacons also visited the sick and the elderly, delivered Christmas poinsettias, and basically attended to the personal needs of the congregation. We met every month to coordinate all of these activities. The meetings were miserable—three hours of endless policies, procedures and details which, for the most part, were not necessary.

Do we need a form for this? Who will organize that? When can this be approved? It was mind-boggling.

After my first six months on this board, I decided I would try to lasso in the process. I told the moderator of the Deacons that I had an agenda item called "Deacon Meetings" for the next meeting. He unquestioningly added the item to the agenda.

At the meeting, I addressed the lack of efficiency in these meetings and suggested we try to find a way to streamline some of the activities. As I saw numerous heads nodding (not the sleepy kind), I knew I was on the right track. Then came the fun.

I explained to the board that I was *so* committed to having more efficient meetings I would wear a dress and present the moderator with a dozen roses if he ever finished a Deacon meeting in less than one hour. The effect of this proposal on the group surprised even me. From that day on, the moderator and the other Deacons were on a mission to eliminate extraneous discussions, streamline decisions and drive us through the agenda as efficiently as possible. For the next six months our meetings ran from three hours to two hours to 90 minutes to 75 minutes and even as short as 65 minutes. But never once were we able to end in less than one hour.

Of course every time they got close, I just brought up coffee!

*   *   *   *   *

Are you involved in meetings at work, at church, at your children's school, or for your community association? Do you dread going to them? Do they go on for hours and no one does anything about it? Well, maybe you should inject a little humor into the situation and stop taking it so seriously. Don't be afraid to shake things up. Be the someone who gets creative and helps those meetings become fun, productive gatherings everyone looks forward to rather than dreads.

What You See
Is What You Get

One of the great lessons I've learned about humor is it is all around us, in every corner of our lives. If we keep our humor antennae up and look for laughs, we'll find reasons to smile every day. The following are some of my favorite examples of humor that I found just by paying attention. Enjoy.

*   *   *   *   *

On CNBC one morning, the reporter was interviewing the medical director at Hackensack Medical Center in New Jersey. Do you realize there is actually a hospital called "Hack-en-sack"? How would you feel about having surgery there?

*   *   *   *   *

The following appeared in the Herndon Connection Newspaper in Herndon, Virginia (the italics are my favorite parts!):

A Fairfax County police animal control officer responded to the X block of Centreville Road in the

Herndon area on Thursday, Dec 7, for the report of a squirrel running about a woman's home. When the officer *confronted* the squirrel, it leapt off a window ledge and then jumped into an open baby grand piano. Without harming the squirrel, the officer played the piano until the squirrel jumped out of the piano and onto some curtains. The squirrel then jumped onto the officer's head. It stayed there for only a moment before it pounced onto the couch. The squirrel stayed there long enough for the officer to catch him at which time the squirrel was released outside. There was some damage to the curtains; however, *neither the squirrel nor the officer sustained any injuries*. The officer played "All I Want," by Toad the Wet Sprocket from their "Fear" album. (Reprinted with permission of the *Herndon Connection* newspaper.)

* * * * *

A few years ago, I did a training program for the staff of an adult day care facility. This facility provided a place for adults with Alzheimer's disease and other chronic illnesses to be cared for while family members got a break from the day to day care. In between training sessions, I visited the restroom. When I turned to leave the stall, I noticed a big white sign on the door *inside* the stall. The sign said:

DID YOU REMEMBER TO WASH YOUR HANDS?

I understand the purpose of this sign. It was a reminder to the residents to wash their hands before leaving the restroom. But by placing that sign on the inside of the stall, I believe they may have created a worse problem than they solved!

*   *   *   *   *

Because of my experience as a social worker, I am on numerous mailing lists for counselors and therapists. One day, I received a brochure advertising a workshop for those dealing with "Survivors of Traumatic Stress." The brochure arrived in shreds! Apparently, the folks at the Postal Service could benefit from this workshop.

*   *   *   *   *

A number of years ago, I saw a fax cover sheet that had a note at the bottom that read:

Please return this so I have a copy.

YOU HAVE A COPY! YOU SENT IT TO ME. Sorry.

*   *   *   *   *

While driving to my daughter Caitlin's gymnastics meet, I passed a store called "See Thru Windows." Don't you wonder if the executives in this company actually sat around a large boardroom table and considered this name? Do you think the CEO said, "OK, let's see? What could we call our window company? We want them to be sturdy, easy-to-maintain and come in a variety of styles. Oh yeah, and we want them to be see through....wait a minute, that's it!"

*   *   *   *   *

In Lorton, Virginia, a suburb of Washington, DC, there was a maximum security prison. It was part of the Washington, DC prison system and housed pretty tough criminals. The road that runs past the prison is a small two-lane country road that is overburdened by rush hour traffic. One day, I was on my way to a meeting and decided to take this road as a short cut. Little did I know that, due to construction, the traffic was backed up for three miles.

As I inched along, I realized I was going to be late for my meeting. I could feel my blood pressure rising and I started to become tense. I was trapped on this road with no other way to go. I had to just sit there and take it. Then, about a block from the prison, I glanced at a sign in the front yard of a small white farmhouse. The sign said

Prison View Estates

I pounded the steering wheel and burst out laughing. I was concerned about the traffic while this family went to bed every night one block from killers and rapists. I can only imagine that the prison was built after this family had lived there for years. I guess the home-owners didn't want to move and chose to react with a sense of humor instead of a sense of horror. Well done.

* * * * *

Following a conference presentation in Ocean City, Maryland, I was on my way to the restroom when a male participant started talking to me. He had a specific question about my presentation so we agreed to talk on the way to the men's room. As I write this, I realize it is already sounding a bit odd. Men just don't go the restroom together. We shower together in locker rooms, we pat each other on the butt during football games and we cry during Three Stooges movies but we just don't hang out together in restrooms. Women? That's another story.

So, we walk into the restroom together and at the same time, we both stop and look at the urinals. *What's wrong with them?* I thought. For the women out there who don't frequent men's restrooms, let me educate you on the layout. Men have two choices of equipment in public restrooms. These choices match the duties which we must perform. In a typical restroom, there are four to five stalls containing run-of-the-mill toilets. In addition, and this is the bonus, there are also four to five wall mounted porcelain *urinals*. These functional troughs resemble a rectangular box mounted vertically on the wall with a receptacle at the bottom. As the name implies, this item is for urinating. The beauty in this invention is we're not forced to wait for the regular toilet if regular toileting is not what we need to accomplish. Instead, we can use the urinal for a quick pass (so to speak), thus allowing us to limit the time we must socialize with others in the restroom.

At this particular hotel in Ocean City, the urinals were different. They looked like a large porcelain replica of the bottom jaw of a pelican. An oblong, trough mounted to the floor half full of water. As we cautiously approached these unfamiliar receptacles, I said to my new bathroom buddy, "That's a funky looking urinal."

He said, "Yeah, it's like European."

In case you missed the full impact of his comment, repeat it out loud.

I'll give it to you phonetically: "Yeah, it's like 'You're a peein.'"

Wow.

Natural humor just doesn't get any better than that. We looked at each other and laughed. It was definitely a bonding moment (I know. You're thinking, *more bathroom humor*. Don't blame me. It just keeps happening. I promise to keep my antennae up in other places so I can share more living room humor, dining room table humor, and front yard humor too).

*   *   *   *   *

At Kings Dominion Amusement Park near Richmond, Virginia, there is a very nice water park. Several years ago, our family visited the park. My son was enjoying the wading pool. As I stood there watching him, I noticed the following sign written on the deck of the pool:

Six Inches, No Diving

My feeling is if someone needs to know he shouldn't dive in six inches of water, we should allow him to try. I think that's what Darwin had in mind anyway.

*   *   *   *   *

I read about a company customer who had not paid his bill in nine months. The company sent out one more invoice to him that said:

Your payment is 9 months overdue.
We have now carried you longer than your mother.

Allegedly, the bill was paid within two weeks.

*   *   *   *   *

In the book, *The Healing Power of Humor*, author Allen Klein tells the story of a woman who was pulled over for speeding. When the police officer came to her window, she gave him a "Get Out of Jail Free" card from Monopoly! Now that's a great perspective. Not only did she find a way to make the situation more tolerable for herself, it probably made the cop's day.

Once I read about this, I put one of those cards in my car. I haven't been pulled over once since! But I can't wait to use it.

After telling that story in one of my presentations, a woman came up to me and said, "You'll never believe what happened to me. I was 40 years old when I got my first speeding ticket. I was so nervous, and I could tell the cop approaching my car seemed angry. I was fumbling with my license and my registration when he got to my window. I rolled down the window and watched as he flipped open his ticket book. I don't know what possessed me but I said, 'I'll have a cheeseburger and fries.' He looked over the top of his glasses, shook his head in wonder, closed his ticket book and went back to his car."

Now clearly there was a risk involved! The worst thing that could have happened was she would have gotten a ticket anyway. She took a chance on humor though and it was just the ticket to turning things around.

* * * * *

Best-selling children's' book author Dr. Seuss reminds us, "From there to here, from here to there. Funny things are everywhere." It's true. In the most unexpected places, humor is there. You may be thinking, "But I'm not funny." Don't worry. Other people are! Just keep your humor antennae up when watching TV, reading the paper, playing with your kids, and encountering signs and bulletin boards. If you do, you'll fill your days with a-ha's and ha-ha's.

PART IV

HUMOR CONNECTS US WITH OTHERS

Person to Person

*There's nothing like a gleam of humor
to reassure you that a fellow human being
is ticking inside a strange face.*

– Eva Hoffman, author

Therapeutic Humor?

One of the greatest gifts we can give another human being is the gift of laughter. Humor touches our soul and allows us to connect with one another in a deep and meaningful way. And it's just darn fun!

In 1983, while working as a mental health worker at the University of Virginia Medical Center in Charlottesville, Virginia, I was escorting a group of psychiatric patients on a walk outside. This allowed the patients to get a refreshing break from the stifling environment of an inpatient psychiatric unit. On this beautiful fall day, I was the only staff member accompanying five patients. Most of the patients were quite calm, but one was a very challenging adolescent girl who had been placed in the hospital by her parents because of her inability to cope with people in authority. She had rebelled against her teachers, parents and anyone else who asserted any power over her.

A few minutes into the walk, this adolescent girl walked up to me with her hands on her hips and got right up in my face.

She said defiantly, "What would you do if I bolted right now—I just took off running and left the hospital?"

As I contemplated just the right therapeutic response, I looked to see if there were any other staff members around. There weren't. I did notice however that the other four patients had gathered close to hear my response.

I thought for a minute, and with a straight face said to this young girl, "I'm glad you asked because whenever there is only one staff member on a walk with several patients, the hospital equips us with a tranquilizer gun. I'd shoot you in the back of the leg and drag you back to the hospital."

I stood there boldly waiting for her reaction. The look on her face indicated she wasn't sure if I was serious or not. She forced a smile and then stayed about 18 inches from me during the remainder of the walk!

Please understand. I wasn't making fun of this girl and wasn't trying to be rude. Her issue was authority and I was the person in charge, whether I liked it or not. When she challenged me, I could not respond with a typical parental response by saying, "You know it's not right to leave." Instead, I had to come up with another answer. So, I fell back on my own coping style, which is to try something funny.

It worked.

I found out later this frustrated adolescent girl appreciated my response. Rather than giving her the authoritarian direction that would have set her off, I did something different. I think she understood and was grateful that I tried another approach. For the next few weeks, we worked well together because humor had connected us.

Rudderly Ridiculous

One of my good friends, Michael Aronin, is a stand-up comic and professional speaker. He is very funny and one of his unique attributes is he has Cerebral Palsy. I'm no expert on this affliction but it seems that when he was born, there was a brief period of time when no oxygen got to his brain. The result of this air-lessness was that some portions of his brain were damaged. I've tried to convince him there was more damage than he realizes but he denies it.

The damage affected Michael's motor skills and his speech. When he walks, his arms and legs jerk uncontrollably, and he staggers a bit. His speech is not really slurred but it is a bit garbled. Yet he is a successful speaker and he is funny.

When I first met Michael, he was performing a short pre-sentation at the Washington, DC chapter of the National Speakers Association. He blew the audience away. He humor-ously discussed his disability and how humor has helped him to cope. I knew I had to get to know this guy better.

It is not easy for many people to interact with someone like Michael. His speech and unusual movements sometimes em-barrass or inhibit others from approaching him. But Michael has a wonderful gift of acceptance which melts away any of these apprehensions.

Michael and I met for lunch one day to talk about business. Being a former social worker, I was relatively comfortable be-ing with someone who had a disability. I had learned to be open and honest rather than trying to pretend that nothing was dif-ferent. I told Michael right up front, "I will let you do everything yourself unless you ask for my assistance." He appreciated my candor.

We sat down at our table and were greeted by a young wait-ress. She asked for our beverage order and when Michael ordered a Coke with lemon, you could see she was somewhat uneasy with his speech. She left and we continued our conversation. As she was approaching with our drinks, Michael turned his menu around and said, "Watch this."

The waitress served our drinks and Michael said, "'Scuse me, I need a new menu 'cause they printed mine upside down."

The look on her face began with surprise, then concern and then the recognition that Michael was pulling her leg. She started to laugh. She took our order and smiled all the way back to the kitchen. Michael did that. He made her feel comfortable. He caused her to see past his disability to the person underneath it. What a gift.

A couple of years ago, my family booked a Caribbean cruise during the week of our kids' spring break. Two weeks before the cruise, I got an urgent call from my travel agent, Jan. Apparently our boat was broken. The cruise ship we were to sail on had developed a mechanical problem that would take six weeks to repair. Our cruise was cancelled.

The kids were especially disappointed. We had looked forward to this for months and now we weren't going. But the next day, Jan called and said she was able to book us on another cruise line for the same week. She had worked all night on making the change. We were thrilled and still don't know how she did it.

Three days before we left on our cruise, I got a call from Mary Simmons, who worked for our new cruise line. The call went something like this.

"Mr. Culberson, this is Mary Simmons from Carnival Cruises. I don't really know how to say this but the main rudder on your cruise ship is not working properly and has to be replaced. Unfortunately, the rudder is made in Europe and will take several days to get here and then another day or so to install it and test it. We are terribly sorry to inform you that we must cancel your cruise. I hope you understand."

"You have got to be kidding me," I replied. "This is the second time this has happened. My daughter cried the first time and I can't believe you're telling me this is happening again."

"I understand, Mr. Culberson."

"No, I don't think you do understand. This is not acceptable. I am very upset and this will cause a great deal of unhappiness for me and my family. How can you do this to us only two days before our cruise?"

As I prepared myself for several minutes of berating this Carnival representative, she said, "Ron?"

I didn't even take a breath. "I want to talk with someone in a higher position. I will not stand for this. I have rights, you know."

"Ron?"

"Uh, what?"

"Ron, this is Tease."

"Who?"

"Tease Aronin, Michael's wife. Got ya!"

I had been had.

Michael came up with the idea and the two of them developed the script. They completely fooled me. It was hilarious but I *did* burst a blood vessel in my head when I was yelling at her.

When I see comedians or humorists, I always wonder what they are like in real life. Are they naturally funny or have they just developed great material? Michael Aronin lives his message. He is not only a funny person, he lives like one. It is his ability to use humor to connect with others that makes him so accessible. I'm grateful to call him a friend.

* * * * *

Can you think of a time someone's sense of humor helped you see past their exterior? This person made you laugh or smile, and at that moment, they were not 300 pounds, or five feet tall, or born with a birth mark. They were not light skinned, dark skinned, American, Mexican or Asian. He or she was simply a human being with whom you were sharing a laugh. That's the power of humor. It connects us from the inside out.

Marching Orders

*In the judgment, a man will be held accountable
for every blessing he refused to enjoy.*

– Jewish Proverb

Victor Borge once said, "Laughter is the shortest distance between two people." I know this to be true, and yet there are those who just won't allow themselves to enjoy the joy of humor. I want to be around those who appreciate it. I have always tried to make it a part of my life, yet others seem to spend their time trying to get rid of it.

I was in the band. There, I said it. This was one of the great dilemmas in life. Being musical was cultured. Being musical was educational. Being musical was valued. But being in the band was definitely not cool. I originally played the trumpet. The trumpet is kinda cool. Trombones are pretty cool. The drums are really cool. The oboe is not cool. Neither is the French horn or the clarinet. So I was reasonably happy playing my sort-of cool trumpet. Then one day in eighth grade, my third year in band, the band director came up to me and made me an offer I couldn't refuse. He suggested I switch to baritone horn. His entire offer was based on two issues: For one, he thought I would like it better; second was my lips were too big to hit the high notes on my trumpet. The baritone horn used a larger mouthpiece which was better suited for those of us with big boned lips. So I switched. A year or so later, as I sat and watched the straining neck muscles of the first chair trumpet player, I decided it was definitely a good move.

High school band can be a lot of fun but it is also a curse. Let's face it; I was very unlikely to have a date outside the band. Who's going to date a band guy and a baritone player at that? Band was just not high school cool. It was grandmother or PBS cool, and you know how well those go over in high school. But I stuck with it, thinking if I got good, I might have a future in music. These are the plans you have when you are 14—before you discover parties, alcohol and girls.

The fun part of band was I got to go on some pretty cool trips. My high school band—the Patrick Henry Rebel Band—marched at Disney World in Florida. We played *It's a Small World* 32 times as we high stepped our way along the spectator clad streets of the Magic Kingdom on a very typical Florida summer day. The temperature was pushing 100 degrees, and guess what we were wearing? Lovely navy and royal blue, 100% wool uniforms, complete with tall, fuzzy Q-tip-esque hats.

Even in the midst of one of the coolest places you could ever be, our nerdy band-ness came through. We lost five members that day to heat exhaustion. It was not a pretty sight. Minnie Mouse had to carry one of the members to the first aid station while the others spent the next couple of days in their hotel rooms. Nonetheless, I am still proud to say I marched at Disney World.

I was lucky in both high school and college because we had crummy football teams. Therefore, the band was appreciated. In my last year of high school, our varsity team had lost 41 games in a row. If we had lost one more game, we would have set a national record for consecutive losses. Of course we didn't. We won. The fans rushed the field as if we had beaten Florida State. I sat in the stands thinking, *1-41 is not nearly as cool as being the losingest team in high school sports would have been*. But come to think of it, I was in the BAND of a 1-41 team!

After all of the rehearsals, week-long band camps, yearly concerts and numerous competitions, I realized that even though I was good (first alternate baritone in the 1979 Virginia State Band Competition), I did not see myself spending too much of my future in music. That changed when I was accepted for admission at the University of Virginia.

I had applied to UVA by early decision so I found out I was accepted in my senior year. Later that spring I received a letter with a return address that said, "AWUVAFCIOPMPBCSRU." I opened the letter and found I had been invited to join the *Award Winning University of Virginia Fighting Cavalier Indoor/Outdoor Precision Marching Pep Band and Chowder Society Review Unlimited!* I was intrigued, so I read on.

The University of Virginia is steeped in tradition. Thomas Jefferson founded it and the way the faculty and students refer to his foundership, you feel as if he is still there. The campus is called "The Grounds" rather than the campus; the new students are "first-year" rather than freshmen; the diplomas are the size of my driveway; and instead of a marching band, they had the AWUVAFCIOPMPBCSRU or the "Pep Band" for short.

The Pep Band was very different from a typical marching band. It was a scramble style band, modeled after the Ivy League bands, in which the members run chaotically around the football field forming pictures, telling jokes and playing cool songs.

As I read the letter of invitation, I felt like this band was hipper than my wool and Q-tip high school band. So, I sent a letter of interest and a few weeks later, got an invitation to audition during my first week of school.

I arrived at my audition feeling similar to when I auditioned in regional and state competitions. The difference this time was I really wanted to succeed. I wanted to be in the UVA Pep Band.

I auditioned for the director, the conductor and a fourth-year baritone horn player, all of whom were students. I only missed a few notes and I felt good about my performance. I was then asked to complete a short application which included questions about my musical background (I left out the part about my big lips), my direction of study and my contact information. The last line asked, "Do you have anything else to add?" In an attempt to make sure I got a spot in this non-traditional humor-focused band, I gave a non-traditional humorous answer. I listed ten numbers and added them up! I know, it's off the clever scale.

Three days later, I found out I had been accepted as a member of the band. I was a bit full of myself thinking my sharp-witted number thing had made the difference. It wasn't until my fourth year in college that I found out the auditions were not completely what they seemed. The band accepted just about anyone who wanted to join. The male director, our conductor and one of the baritone horn players held the auditions to see if there were any good looking women joining the band. And I thought I was so clever.

The Pep Band's mission was simple. Entertain with satire and a bit of relatively well-played music. Each show had four-to-five pre-game jokes and eight-to-ten halftime jokes with a bunch of songs and the National Anthem thrown in for good measure. The format was simple: Make a formation; tell a joke; play a song. The challenge was that the jokes had to be current *and* funny.

For instance, in 1978, the governor of Maryland had been indicted on some sort of corruption charges. I think his name was Marvin Mandel. When the University of Virginia played *at* the University of Maryland that year, the band introduced its special guest conductor as "the Honorary Marvin Mandel." Out came a band member dressed in a striped outfit with a ball and chain attached to one ankle. The band received a standing ovation from the Maryland fans, but was banned (so to speak) from performing at the University of Maryland ever again. Legend has it the acting Governor called the Governor of Virginia and asked for a formal apology. From the band's perspective, it didn't get any better than that.

One year we were playing our arch rivals, Virginia Tech. During the halftime performance, our band-member PA announcer said, "We interrupt this halftime performance to bring you this special announcement. Last night, Virginia Tech's library burned down. Both books were lost.......and one wasn't even colored in yet."

The band then scrambled into the shape of a building and played *Disco Inferno*!

The Virginia Tech band got even a year or so later. We were playing *at* Virginia Tech and when the Tech band strutted past us in their military style formation, we started chanting "High School Band! High School Band!" To our amazement and deep respect, their band turned to us and shouted, "High School Team. High School Team!" That year, we gave *them* a standing ovation.

Controversy always surrounded the Virginia Pep Band because there were alumni who never liked the humor. They wanted a formal marching band with uniforms, flags and boring company fronts. The students however, wanted the rich tradition and humor of the Pep Band. But as the years went on, the pressure from the alumni took its toll. After the Maryland incident, the athletic department instituted a censoring process on the shows. Each Thursday before the Saturday game, a group of band members met with the athletic director and let him read the planned show. He would "eliminate" the jokes that were not acceptable. Those eliminated usually had sexual references or took a cheap shot at some public figure. Although the censoring limited the creativity, they had still put together some awesome shows.

When Virginia played the University of Tennessee at the 1991 Sugar Bowl, a band member dressed like Elvis came out onto the field and the entire band jumped on top of him. The announcer said, "Now, can we all agree that Elvis is really dead?" The Tennessee fans revolted and once again Virginia's governor was asked for an apology. Some people just didn't appreciate the humor.

Eventually, the band was prevented from doing halftime shows. In 2003, a wealthy alumnus gave $1.5 million to start a real band and the band was *dis*-band-ed. It's sad. The formations, the humor and the music were a tradition that made our games unique. We gave the crowd an opportunity to laugh. We tried to show people that we do not have to get so caught up in the seriousness of our world all the time. But that attitude was a threat to some and as a result, the humor was silenced.

Ultimately, I realized my band was cool and those that disliked us were not. So there.

*   *   *   *   *

Not everyone will share your style of humor, so we need to look for people who do. And there will be those who will try to sabotage your attempts to make things fun. Have fun and laugh anyway. They can't take away your laughter. We each have our own humor profile, our own fun DNA. Not everyone matches. So once you find people who laugh at the same things you do, band together. Now *that's* cool.

Dam!

He deserves paradise he who
makes his companions laugh.

– The Koran

Humor is a powerful way to get a message across. It brings a point home and creates a wonderful experience for the listeners.

A couple of years ago, we went to Las Vegas for our family vacation. Even though our kids were seven and ten, we had heard Las Vegas had become "family friendly" and there were lots of activities that would be fun for the whole fam damily. Interestingly, a few years after our trip, the hotels in Las Vegas discovered they weren't making enough money on families, as this took parents' time away from gambling. So they ditched the idea and returned to the decadent adult entertainment "strip" that made Vegas famous.

On our trip, we looked forward to seeing the Hoover Dam, the Grand Canyon and a number of amusement parks in Vegas. I would play golf, my wife and I would gamble and we would all get our fill of the cheap buffets. It sounded like a great plan and to this day, our kids remember it as one of their best vacations.

Shortly after we arrived, we discovered Las Vegas is not very warm in March. Even though it's sitting in the middle of the desert, it's cold in the early spring.

The day we drove to the Grand Canyon, it was chilly but a lovely day nonetheless. We took the five-hour trip on the desolate Arizona highways. In fact, during one stretch of road, we didn't see a gas station for 30 miles. This made us realize how much we take for granted back home in the suburbs of Washington, DC.

We arrived at the Grand Canyon, and although the clear blue skies had clouded over, it was still an unbelievable sight. It was almost too much to take in. The dramatic colors, the depth of the canyon walls and the sheer magnitude of this work of nature were totally captivating. I could have looked at it for hours. But my kids couldn't. After about 15 minutes, they wanted to do something else.

"Let's go eat," said my daughter.

"Look at that funny car," said my son.

"Eat? Car?" I yelled, "This is the Grand Canyon. Do you realize we're on sacred ground here? This is not something you get to see every day. Don't you appreciate what you're looking at?"

I *was* the stereotypical father. I looked down to make sure I wasn't wearing shorts with black socks. How could I be like this? I was only 40 and 40 is not very old. In fact Michael Jordon was only 38 and he was still playing in the NBA. But even though I was 40, I sounded like I was 60. No offense to those of you over 60, but when you turn 60, things change. At 60, you've replaced MTV with NPR. Your pants have more elastic in them. The only magazine you can read is the *Reader's Digest* . . . Large Print Edition.

But at 40, I was still listening to rock and roll, I loved my Levis and I could understand the vernacular of young people. So how come all of the sudden I sounded like I was 60?

My wife gave me that "It's useless" look and I resigned myself to the fact that we would be spending the next hour eating in the lodge and shopping in the Grand Canyon gift shop.

Maybe that's not so bad, I thought, *I might be able to find a nice book on the history of the Canyon.*

We went to the restaurant. Luckily, the Grand Canyon is part of the US Department of the Interior rather than a private tourist attraction like Disney World or Universal Studios. The prices of the food were reasonable and there were no *Canyon Cajun Fries* or the *Grandest Burger in Town*. The meal was actually quite good and the gift shop was fascinating.

After filling our stomachs and emptying our wallets, we decided to go back to the main attraction. The minute we walked out of the lodge, we were aware that the earlier cloud cover had gotten lower and darker. It looked like it might rain.

"Let's go quickly," I said, "so we get to see as much as possible."

Then, the unthinkable happened. The clouds fell below the rim of the canyon and it started snowing.

Snowing? It's the end of March, we're in Arizona and it's snowing!

We went to the edge of the canyon and all we could see was gray snowy fog. We couldn't see ten feet in front of us.

At that point, I felt like Clark Griswald's family in National Lampoon's *Vacation*. He was so intent on getting to Wally World that when he got to the Grand Canyon on the way, he said, "OK, that's nice, let's go." We had enjoyed all of 15 minutes of the Grand Canyon. We had driven five hours, eaten US Park Service food and all we got was 15 minutes of the most amazing hole in the world. I was bummin'.

Knowing the fog was not going to lift, we took our funeral procession to the car and prepared for the long ride back to Vegas.

The next day, we decided to go to the Hoover Dam. The dam is only 45 minutes from Vegas, so the trip was much quicker.

The Hoover Dam is an amazing facility. It was built in 1935 and was finished ahead of schedule and under budget. Can you imagine something like that today? Forget it.

Since it's such a large man-made structure and because of its importance as a source of electricity for much of the southwest, security was very tight. To reduce the risk of bringing in a bomb, no one was allowed to carry a bag into the dam. There were security guards from the parking garage into the building, making sure no one was smuggling anything explosive.

We were so disoriented by the security guards; we weren't really paying attention to the signs in the building. So we walked up to the first counter we saw.

A woman sitting behind the counter looked up and said, "Do you want to go on the *dam* tour?"

Startled, my wife and I looked at each other and assumed we had misunderstood.

"Pardon me?" I said.

"Do you want to go on the dam tour?"

Again, my wife gave me the evil eye and I turned one last time and said, "Excuse me?"

The woman said, "Do you want a ticket for the dam tour?"

Flustered, I said, "Well, hell yes!"

In Hoover Dam world, this use of the word dam is a little inside joke. I think it's wonderful even though it surprised me a bit. Throughout the tour, whenever anyone would stray from the group, the guide would say, "Hey, get back on the dam tour." It was hilarious.

The Hoover Dam is part of the US Park Service. It says a lot to see that even in the federal government; employees can have a little purposeful fun in their work. If government workers can find something in their jobs, you can find something funny in yours. It may take some searching, but it will be *dam* well worth it.

* * * * *

While we should never be purposely offensive, there are times when we can generate good will by being just a bit "naughty." The play on words the Hoover Dam employees used was funny just because it was unexpected. The surprise was funny and we never asked ourselves whether we were offended. We were having too much fun to worry. Whether work, play or falling in love, life isn't supposed to be so dam (!) serious. Lighten up!

Everybody's Doing It

Don't follow the path. Go off the path
and create your own trail.

– Ralph Waldo Emerson, philosopher

Many of you might not be able to figure out how to add more humor into the way you interact with others. Look at how these folks did it and perhaps you can follow their examples.

Not Doubtful in the Least

After a presentation to the American Cancer Society, I was approached by a woman who wished to share a funny story with me. She explained that while she was going through radiation and chemotherapy—not particularly funny experiences, mind you—she lost all of her hair. She admitted she was not embarrassed by her bald head, but quickly realized others were. So, on most days, she wore a scarf to cover her baldness.

When invited to a Halloween costume party, this woman could not decide on a costume that worked well with the scarf. So here's what she did: She painted her head black and then painted a giant white "8" on the back of her head! She went to the party as one of those magic eight balls that use the floating triangle to answer your ponderous questions with ridiculously mysterious answers like "Maybe yes" or "It's possible." Then, on several pieces of paper, she wrote out these answers, put tape on the back and kept them in her hand. All night long she would walk up to people and tell them to ask her a question. Then, she'd shake her head and slap an answer on her forehead.

It was brilliant.

This courageous woman believed in the concept of *it's not what happens to you but how you react*. She transformed her disadvantage into a distinct advantage by allowing others to laugh with her and her unusual "head" case.

Pepto Dismal

The CEO of a company once asked the senior management team to review a state-of-the-industry report and to give him feedback by an agreed upon date. When the date came, the CEO had not received any feedback. He was furious. He informed the group that after his two-week vacation, things were going to change on the management team. He said he was going to "raise the bar" and those that didn't rise to the occasion would be in serious trouble.

The senior staff was anxious to say the least. They knew that they had let their CEO down but they also felt he had over-reacted. For two weeks they worried about the staff meeting where he would announce his plans.

The big day arrived and the CEO marched into the conference room to address the issues he had raised two weeks prior. Much to his surprise, the conference room tables were full of Pepto Bismol, Rolaids, Tums and dozens of other antacids. The staff, in a fun way, had shown him how anxious they were. He burst out laughing and acknowledged their anxiety. The meeting proceeded with a great deal more understanding on both parts.

More Toilet Humor

While speaking at a conference, a female participant shared the following story with me:

As a single parent, I had warned my son numerous times to put the toilet seat down when he finished using the bathroom. No matter how often I told him, he didn't listen. So, one day, I said, "The next time I find the toilet seat up, I will find you wherever you are and no matter who you're with, I will take you into the bathroom and demand that you put the seat down."

Sure enough, the next time I found the toilet seat up, my son was entertaining some friends from school. I went in and told him to follow me. As he walked behind me, friends in tow, I led him to the bathroom. In my most serious parent voice, I demanded, "Put that toilet seat down!"

My son bent over the toilet and said, "Toilet seat, you're ugly."

Is that great or what? This woman said his comment totally disarmed her and the only thing she could do was laugh. Even in the midst of life's stresses, a childlike attitude can smooth over the rough edges.

If You Can't Say Something Nice...

I mentioned earlier that The Barter Theater is known as the "state theater" of Virginia. Located in Abingdon, Virginia, this quaint, yet beautifully renovated theater has attracted talented actors since 1933. Ernest Borgnine and Ned Beatty have both performed on the stage of the Barter Theater and it has a national reputation for outstanding shows.

Robert Porterfield, the founder of the Barter Theater, used to begin every performance by welcoming the audience to his theater. A consummate professional, yet also a businessman, he would complete his welcome by saying, "If you like what you see tonight, please talk about us. If you don't, then keep your mouth shut!"

Humor Is in Your Blood

Ed Gulnac has a master's degree in Guidance and Counseling. He was the Executive Director of a residential treatment center for some of the most difficult youth in Erie, Pennsylvania.

Ed was leading a group counseling session when one young man became angry, stormed out of the room, went through the kitchen and out the back door of the building. Ed ran out the front door to cut the guy off in the driveway.

The young man had picked up a butcher knife in the kitchen when he met Ed in the driveway and he held the knife out in a threatening way.

The residents in this facility had served time in jail, so stabbing a counselor was not out of the question—even though it would result in being sent back to prison for a much longer time. Ed had a black belt in karate and could easily take the knife away from the young man but he knew the kid had potential and did not want to see him go to jail. So Ed knew he had to do something before the young man made any move towards stabbing him.

Ed had gotten married a few weeks before and the shirt he was wearing was a gift from his new wife. He said to the young man, "Have you ever tried to get blood out of a shirt?"

"What the hell did you say?" the kid responded.

"Have you ever tried to get blood out of a shirt? If you stab me, my wife will be so upset about your getting blood on my new shirt, she will hunt you down."

The thought of this ludicrous idea caused the young man to burst out laughing. He handed the knife back to Ed. After a soda and a long talk, the situation was better and the young man remained in the residential program for further treatment.

"If it hadn't been for humor, he would have been in jail, one of us would have been moderately hurt and the other one would have had serious injuries." Ed said. "Humor saved the day for both of us."

It Tastes Like Chicken

It had been a stressful drive to the airport, during which I got lost and barely made it to my plane on time. I had just settled into my seat on an afternoon flight from Seattle to Washington, DC, The pilot came on the loudspeaker and said this:

Good afternoon ladies and gentleman and welcome to our flight to Washington Dulles Airport. Our flying time today will be four hours and forty minutes. After we reach our cruising altitude, our cabin crew will be coming through the cabin with beverage service. After that, they'll be serving a hot meal. Tonight you have two choices. You can have Chicken Kiev or meatloaf. Let me just say that there are a limited number of each entrée. Let me apologize in advance if we run out of your choice before we get to your row. But between you and me…it all tastes the same anyway.

The cabin erupted with laughter. And no one complained. Just so you know, I got the meatloaf. Funny thing, it tasted like chicken!

It's All in the Delivery

A friend of our family, Bill Platt, used to be a pharmaceutical salesperson. To make his sales calls a bit more interesting, he learned several magic tricks that he would use prior to pitching a particular item.

On one visit to a physician's office, Bill placed a small foam rubber rabbit in his hand. He closed his hand, opened it again and magically, there were several rabbits in his hand. He then began his sales pitch for the contraceptives that his company offered.

It's magic when you use humor for your advantage!

*   *   *   *   *

Are you thinking, "Come on Ron, it's easy for you! You love your job, you get to travel to these exotic places, you have a brilliant, beautiful wife and bright, interesting children and you're involved in your church and community, so you know your life matters. No wonder you have fun. You have a lot to smile about."

You're right. I do have a wonderful life and I'm grateful for it. But not all of these people have had wonderful lives. Some have more to be unhappy about than happy about.

But they chose to have a sense of humor anyway. If you use humor to deflate the difficulty, humor will become your saving grace. Can you do that even during tough times?

PART V

IN THE END, HUMOR HELPS

Dying for a Good Laugh

Life does not cease to be funny
when people die just as it does not cease
to be serious when people laugh.

– George Bernard Shaw, playwright

We're near the end of the book and there is much more that could be said. Similarly, when we near the end of our lives, there is still more that could be done. Life and death commingle just as joy and tragedy does. And laughter can sustain us even in times of death and dying.

On December 5, 1984, my seven-year-old nephew Allen died of a brain tumor. The days following his death were a blur of activities. The busy-ness of making arrangements, greeting friends and sharing memories kept us conveniently distracted so our brains would not stumble into the pools of grief scattered throughout our mind. We would swim in those pools enough over months ahead, so the distractions were welcomed.

After two viewings, a memorial service and a graveside service, our family gathered for a meal at my parents' home. We picked at our dinner, a generously donated gift of the usuals. Chicken Tetrazine, green-bean casserole with the little canned onion rings on top, buttery homemade rolls and rich chocolate brownies made from scratch. Then we slumped into any seat available in the living room. We looked like warriors who had just returned from battle. Our eyes showed the fatigue of defeat. Then, for the next two hours, we told jokes.

In retrospect, this seems crazy. It even hints of disrespect, and yet no one protested. Was it wrong? Were we teetering on the edge of sanity? Not at all. We were feeling the effects of grief overload and needed a well-deserved break. Not a break that was disrespectful or cruel, but a healing break that would allow us to face our grief the next morning with renewed strength. We knew the days ahead would be full of reminders of the loss we had experienced, but in that moment in my parents' living room, the laughter gave us the strength to go on.

After ten years in hospice care, I am quite comfortable with the issue of death. I don't welcome death but I am not intimidated by it either. Part of that comes from experience and part of it comes from my faith. Nonetheless, most people in our society are not even comfortable talking about death. I find this fascinating. Of all the things we can experience in life, the one we are most certainly going to experience is death. Yet we can't discuss it and we definitely can't mix humor with it.

At Henny Youngman's funeral, the rabbi leading the service said, "God, take Henny Youngman, please." This was a reference to the line Youngman used in much of his comedy routine, "take my wife, please." It was brilliant and it captured the essence of both Henny Youngman's career and his death. It was neither disrespectful nor was it silly. The humor was a nice break to the normal funeral routine.

There is a Chinese proverb that says, "You cannot prevent the birds of sorrow from flying over your head but you can prevent them from building nests in your hair." This is the truth in life *and* death. We must take the good and the bad but not be consumed by the bad. Humor is a part of life and it is no less a part of death, except that our culture does not typically embrace it during that difficult time.

In hospice care, the focus is on quality, not quantity of life. Hospice workers often refer to the *life in your days* rather than *the days in your life*. This captures the essence of life and it's so important if we are going to get to the end of our life with a sense of satisfaction and accomplishment.

When I worked in hospice care, there was a wonderful volunteer named Kathy. She always searched the obituaries to find those individuals who had designated hospice as the recipient of donations. She would cut out these obituaries and give them to our fundraising department, so the proper acknowledgments could be made. But Kathy was also working for me. She would search the obituaries for funny entries and pass those on to me! It was great. I had my own death/humor scavenger.

One obituary said Mr. Thompson had "gone to be with Jesus in his home in Palmyra." I'm surprised this did not cause a sudden horde of bus tours to the "new" holy land in Palmyra!

Another obituary appeared on April 14 but said the woman died in her sleep on *April 17*! We thought we should warn her!

My favorite was an entry about a woman who appeared to be about 85 to 90 years old. The obituary read, "She was known for her graciousness and sense of humor. Towards the end, her respirations assisted but breathing with difficulty, she said, 'Is there any oxygen loose in the room I'm not getting? Perhaps there is some trapped in the bedclothes'!"

How great is that? Here, a woman is near death and can still share a bit of absurd humor. This is a gift with which we should all be blessed.

So why do we resist it? Is it for fear of offending someone? Is it because we are so sad or distressed? Perhaps we feel it is irreverent. Whatever the reason, we miss the opportunity to enjoy a buffer and a balance to the challenges of death. Rather than focusing on the death itself, we should be focusing on the beauty of the life and the fun's that's still to be had.

Lila Green, in *Making Sense of Humor*, said, "Time flies whether you're having fun or not." When we approach our own death, we most likely will feel the same way. I like what Kermit the Frog said, "Time's fun when you're having flies."

It's all in the perspective.

*   *   *   *   *

How will you face the end of your life? Will it be with grace and humor or will it be with kicking and screaming? Chances are we will face our death in the same way we face our lives. Perhaps there is room in both for a little more humor.

The Punch Line

*Give me, Lord, a soul that knows nothing of
boredom, groans and sighs. Never let me be overly
concerned for this inconstant thing I call me. Lord,
give me a sense of humor so that I may take some
happiness from this life and share it with others.*

– Saint Thomas More

A few months ago, my wife had a hysterectomy. Her gynecologist discovered cysts during an exam for abdominal pain. After several diagnostic tests, we were told the cysts might be cancerous. Wendy opted for the hysterectomy as a way to avoid similar problems in the future.

After the surgery, we were relieved to find out that instead of cancer, she had endometriosis, a condition in which the tissue that lines the uterus grows outside of the uterus. Although the condition is painful, it is usually treatable. The day after the surgery, Wendy was eating, walking, urinating and waiting for the one final sign that the recovery process was "moving" along as it should. That sign was flatulence. All she had to do was pass gas, pass wind, cut the cheese or fart and she was on her way home. What a lovely goal!

My wife's family of origin has always referred to gas passing as "dooting." I don't know how that began and I am somewhat afraid to ask. Nonetheless, my kids have adopted that term as well. When I explained to our children that as soon as mom doots, she could go home, my nine-year-old son Ryan asked, "Who listens for it?"

I envisioned a nurse whose only job was to patrol the post-surgery unit listening for doots. Of course, she would be the Dootician (Sorry for the final time).

Ryan's comment in the midst of a challenging family experience only goes to show we *can* see our glasses *laugh* full. Humor abounds in this world, yet we're so often distracted by the stresses around us, we fail to see it. We must remove our blinders, open our eyes and allow ourselves to receive this gift of humor as a blessing in our lives. By doing so, a new world will open up for us. No kidding!

It's my sincere hope that this book has been fun to read, and it has helped you understand the critical role humor plays in our lives. What I hope most of all is that you are motivated to find your own humor. I hope you build your own joke library. I hope you look for people who share your sense of humor so you can band together with kindred souls. I hope you lighten up instead of tighten up so stress no longer gets the best of you. I hope you learn not to take yourself and others so seriously. I hope that, when you experience emotional or physical pain, you seek comic relief. In essence, I hope from this day forward, you strive to have more fun in your life and work.

So, until we meet again,

May you grow older but never grow up.
May you laugh when the world is not laughing with you.
May the force of milk out your nose be with you.
May your bladder withstand your laughter.
May you never act your age.
May you wipe that smile back *on* your face.
And may you live happily ever laughter.

About the Author

Ronald P. (Ron) Culberson has spent twenty years studying the benefits of humor and laughter. For a decade he was a hospice social worker and manager. He now "works" as a professional speaker and humorist sharing his humor-full message with audiences all over the world. He lives in Herndon, Virginia with his wife Wendy, son Ryan, daughter Caitlin and loyal dog Harley (named after his other "child," a Harley Davidson 1200 Sportster).

For more information on other
products and services:

FUNsulting, etc.
www.funsulting.com
(703) 742-8812